DESSERTS FOR THE NINETIES

Presented By

California Home Economics Teachers

Edited By
Gerry Murry Henderson

Graphics By
Robert Knies Design, Inc.

© Library of Congress Catalog
Card No. 83-072744
ISBN 0-914159-06-2

© California Cookbook Company
1115 Sheppard Drive, Fullerton, California 92631

DESSERTS FOR THE NINETIES

When I was a little boy in Stamford, Texas (town of 4,000—you probably never heard of it!), coming back to the farm house after completing the chores, my favorite question was "what's for dessert, Mom?" (Never mind the meal...just what's THE DESSERT!)

I must tell you that I had a certain "tinge of guilt" when we began publishing this book on desserts because everyone these days is so "health conscious"! And yet most of the California Home Economics Teachers who wrote all these recipes herein agreed that "everybody still loves desserts!" Whether entertaining or celebrating birthdays or anniversaries or just plain fixin' a meal for somebody special—you can always use a good dessert recipe!

Having worked with these California Home Economics Teachers for about 15 years now, I can tell you that they're "somebody special"! These are professional home economists, who teach nutrition and life-skills in California Schools. (Note their names, schools, and towns beneath each recipe).

Certain people work diligently each year to make these books possible: Doug Herrema of Huntington Beach, who continues to come up with "new ideas" for publications; Doug Pierce of Los Angeles, who travels the entire State of California gathering recipes; Bill Horton, Sr. of Canyon Lake, who found this job more fun than retirement! Ingrid Stracky, of Placentia, who is our Office Manager and who taught me that a computer can handle recipes! (This is a long story and you don't want to hear the rest of it!) Glenn Bickford of La Habra, drives all over California, delivering books like the "pony express!"

Our annual editor, Gerry Murry Henderson, of La Verne (teaches at Temple City High School) continues to be our "chief cook" when it comes to "tracking" the ingredients and directions and making sure they correlate. Each year I am increasingly more thankful for an editor like Gerry Henderson!

Robert Knies of Knies Design, Inc. in Fullerton did the artwork and color film processing and designed the front and back covers. He understands marketing and we all say "Thanks, Bob!"

The "living color" throughout the book comes from: Baskin Robbins, Bridgford Foods, Pillsbury, M & M Mars Company, and Hershey's. Our sincere thanks to these companies for their participation.

And last but not least, I'd like to thank you as the purchaser and consumer! We, of California Cookbook Company, appreciate your support, as well as hundreds of schools who sell these books to raise funds. Thank you!

GRADY W. REED, OWNER
CALIFORNIA COOKBOOK COMPANY

P.S. PLEASE NOTE THE REORDER PAGE IN THE BACK OF THE COOKBOOK!

CONTENTS

On Our Front Cover: "Heavenly Chocolate Sundae Cups", page 90 (compliments of Baskin Robbins, Glendale, California).

COLOR PHOTOGRAPHY CREDITS

Interior Photographs, Courtesy of:

Baskin Robbins Ice Cream, Glendale, California, Bridgford Foods Corporation, Anaheim, California, Hershey Foods Corporation, Hershey, Pennsylvania, M & M Mars Company, Accomac, Virginia, Pillsbury Foods Corporation, Minneapolis, Minnesota.

CALIFORNIA HOME ECONOMICS
TEACHERS ADVISORY COMMITTEE

Anderson, Jill
Santa Paula High School, Santa Paula

Banicevich, Gerry
Cordova Sr. High School,
Rancho Cordova

Black-Eacker, Ellen
Nogales High School, La Puente

Blass, Sue
Valhalla High School, El Cajon

Delap, Carol
Goldenwest High School, Visalia

Estes, Marianne
La Mirada High School, La Mirada

Ford, Pam
Temecula Valley High School, Temecula

Geer, Donna
Chino High School, Chino

Glennan, Renee
Sequoia Jr. High School, Simi Valley

Henderson, Gerry
Temple City High School, Temple City

Hibma, Grace
Office of Los Angeles County
Superintendent of Schools, Consultant,
Consumer & Homemaking Education

Himenes, Peggy
Actis Jr. High School, Bakersfield

Hulen, Donna Lyn
Los Alamitos High School,
Los Alamitos

Jones, Dotti
Etiwanda High School, Etiwanda

Lash, Mary
Paramount High School, Paramount

Lundy, Jeri
Grossmont High School, La Mesa

Lopez, Karen
San Luis Obispo High School
San Luis Obispo

Matsuno, Dale
Montebello Intermediate School,
Montebello

Mitchell, Eudora
Valley View High School,
Moreno Valley

Pendleton, Susie
Cerritos High School, Cerritos

Phipps, Louise
Washington Middle School, Vista

Pereira, Marilyn
Hanford High School, Hanford

Priestley, Roberta
Alhambra High School,
Alhambra

Pringle, Adrienne
Royal High School, Simi Valley

Richmond, Mary E.
San Luis Obispo High School,
San Luis Obispo

Ruth, Lynda
La Mirada High School, La Mirada

Sheats, Dianne
Gridley High School, Gridley

Shepherd, Maxine
Moreno Valley High School,
Moreno Valley

Shrock, Bonnie
Kearny High School, San Diego

Titus, Karen
Fullerton College, Fullerton

Traw, Marianne
Ball Jr. High School, Anaheim

Wells, Betty
Oroville High School, Oroville

Wetzel, Naomi
Delta High School, Clarksburg

Whitten, Kathryn P.
Regional Supervisor Home
Economics Education, Fresno

Wildermuth, Ellie
La Canada High School, La Canada

Cakes and Frostings

FROSTING FOR GERMAN CHOCOLATE CAKE

Covers one cake

3/4 cup evaporated milk
1/2 cup brown sugar, packed
1/2 cup sugar
1/2 cup margarine

1 teaspoon vanilla flavoring
3 egg yolks, beaten
1 1/3 cups coconut
1 cup walnuts, chopped

Place the first five ingredients into a saucepan. Bring the mixture to a boil and remove the pan from the heat. Add the beaten egg yolks; stir and bring the mixture to a boil again. Remove from heat. Stir in the coconut and walnuts. Cool the mixture slightly before spreading it on the cake.

"This recipe makes an excellent topping for German Chocolate Cake or any chocolate cake. It's easy to make!"

Bonnie Landin   **Garden Grove High School, Garden Grove**

CHOCOLATE PRALINE LAYER CAKE

Serves 12

1/2 cup butter or margarine
1/4 cup whipping cream
1 cup brown sugar, firmly packed
3/4 cup pecans, coarsely chopped
1 package Pillsbury Plus Devil's
   Food Cake Mix
1 1/4 cups water
1/3 cup oil
3 eggs

Topping:
1 3/4 cups whipping cream
1/4 cup powdered sugar
1/4 teaspoon vanilla
whole pecans, if desired
chocolate curls, if desired

Heat oven to 325 degrees. In a small heavy saucepan, combine butter, 1/4 cup whipping cream, and brown sugar. Cook over low heat just until butter is melted, stirring occasionally. Pour into two (8 or 9") round cake pans; sprinkle evenly with chopped pecans. In large bowl, combine cake mix, water, oil, and eggs at low speed until moistened; beat 2 minutes at highest speed. Carefully spoon batter over pecan mixture. Bake at 325 degrees for 35 to 45 minutes or until cake springs back when touched lightly in center. Cool 5 minutes. Remove from pans and cool completely.

In small bowl, beat 1 3/4 cups whipping cream until soft peaks form. Blend in powdered sugar and vanilla; beat until stiff peaks form. To assemble cake, place 1 layer on serving plate, praline side up. Spread with 1/2 of whipped cream. Top with second layer, praline side up; spread top with remaining whipped cream. Garnish with whole pecans and chocolate curls, if desired. Store in refrigerator.

"So easy to prepare!. So spectacular to serve! So marvelous to eat!"

Pillsbury Bake Off Contest
Grand Prize Winner   **Minneapolis, Minnesota**

GRAMMIE'S CHOCOLATE CAKE

Serves 8

2 tablespoons vegetable oil
1 cup sugar
2 egg yolks, beaten
2 squares unsweetened chocolate
1 cup boiling water, divided

1 teaspoon salt
1½ cups flour
1 teaspoon baking powder
1 teaspoon baking soda

Combine oil and sugar in mixing bowl. Add egg yolks, melted chocolate, and ½ cup boiling water and mix well with spoon. Add salt, flour, and baking powder and mix well. Add soda and remaining ½ cup boiling water. Pour into greased and floured glass 8" square pan (or 6 x 10" glass pan). Bake at 350 degrees for 20 to 25 minutes. Cool and frost with White Mountain Frosting.

"This is my grandmother's recipe which she made for my birthday every year. It's fast and a good size for a small family."

Beth Leighton   **Helix High School, La Mesa**

WHITE MOUNTAIN FROSTING

Frosts a one-layer cake

½ cup sugar
2 tablespoons water
¼ cup light corn syrup

2 egg whites, room temperature
1 teaspoon vanilla

In a saucepan, mix the sugar, water, and corn syrup. Cover and bring to a boil. Cook without the lid to 242 degrees (or 6" thread). Beat egg whites to soft peaks. Gradually pour syrup into egg whites, beating constantly at high speed until stiff peaks form. Add vanilla.

"Great with chocolate cake!"

Beth Leighton   **Helix High School, La Mesa**

BLACK FORREST CHERRY CAKE

Serves 16

1 package devil's food cake mix
1 small bottle maraschino
cherries

1 can cherry pie filling
1 cup whipping cream, whipped
chocolate curls

Prepare and bake cake mix according to package directions for two 9" cake pans. Cool on wire rack. Drain cherries, reserving two tablespoons juice. Sprinkle over one cake layer. Spread with pie filling. Place remaining layer on top. Spread whipped cream over top and side of cake. Decorate with cherries and chocolate curls.

"Most impressive and very easy."

Carleen Topham

Dexter Jr. High School, Whittier

CHOCOLATE NUT TORTE

Serves 8 to 10

1½ cups walnuts or pecans
¾ cup sugar
¼ cup cocoa
¼ cup semisweet chocolate chips
1 teaspoon baking powder
¼ teaspoon baking soda
5 eggs
1 teaspoon vanilla

Chocolate Glaze:
3 ounces (3 squares) semisweet
chocolate
3 tablespoons margarine or
butter
1½ cups powdered sugar
2 tablespoons HOT water
chocolate curls (make curls with
vegetable peeler using room tem-
perature chocolate bar)
powdered sugar

Torte: In food processor, combine nuts, sugar, cocoa, chocolate chips, baking power, and soda; process till nuts are ground. Add eggs and vanilla; process until nearly smooth. Turn into a 9" round cake pan. Cool 10 minutes and remove from pan onto serving plate. Cool completely. Spread with chocolate glaze. Top with chocolate curls piled high. Dust with powdered sugar. Refrigerate until serving time.

Glaze: Melt together the semisweet chocolate and margarine over low heat. Remove from heat; stir in powdered sugar and hot water. Add more water or powdered sugar to make a pouring consistency.

"This is very easy and quick to make and very rich. Everyone says it's sensational!"

Deanne Moody

Monte Vista High School, Spring Valley

CHOCORANGE TORTE

Serves 10 to 12

3 eggs
¾ cup sugar
½ cup all purpose flour
⅓ cup unsweetened cocoa
½ teaspoon baking soda
¼ teaspoon salt

⅓ cup water
1 teaspoon vanilla
Orange Bavarian (recipe follows)
Chocolate Glaze (recipe follows)

Heat oven to 350 degrees. Grease sides and bottom of 9 x 1½'' round pan; line bottom with wax paper. In small mixer bowl, beat eggs 2 minutes at high speed. Gradually add sugar; continue beating 2 minutes. Combine flour, cocoa, baking soda, and salt; add alternately with water and vanilla to mixture. Beat on low speed only until smooth; pour into prepared pan. Bake 25 to 30 minutes or until top springs back when lightly touched in center. Cool 5 minutes, remove from pan and peel off paper. Cool completely. Prepare Orange Bavarian. To assemble torte, place cake layer on serving plate; invert Orange Bavarian onto cake and carefully unmold. Peel off paper; trim edges even with cake. Prepare Chocolate Glaze; pour over torte, allowing glaze to run down sides. Spread quickly over top and sides with spatula for smooth surface; chill several hours or overnight.

Orange Bavarian:
1 envelope unflavored gelatin
¾ cup milk
½ cup sugar
2 eggs, separated
½ cup undiluted frozen orange juice concentrate, thawed

1 teaspoon grated orange peel (optional)
½ teaspoon vanilla
2 tablespoons sugar
½ cup chilled whipping cream

Line bottom of 9 x 1½'' round pan with wax paper. In medium saucepan, sprinkle gelatin over milk; let stand 2 minutes to soften. Add ½ cup sugar and egg yolks to mixture in saucepan; whisk to blend well. Cook over medium heat, stirring constantly, until mixture is very hot and lightly coats a spoon. Do not boil. Remove from heat. Stir orange peel into orange concentrate; add to mixture with vanilla. Cool; chill until mixture begins to set; stirring occasionally. In small mixing bowl, beat egg whites until soft peaks form; gradually add 2 tablespoons sugar and beat until stiff. Gently fold into orange mixture. Beat cream until stiff; carefully fold into mixture. Pour into prepared pan; chill. When completely set, loosen bavarian by running a spatula around pan edge.

Chocolate Glaze:
3 tablespoons butter or margarine
3 tablespoons light corn syrup

1 tablespoon water
1 cup semisweet chocolate chips

In a small saucepan, combine first 3 ingredients; place over medium heat, stirring constantly, until mixture begins to boil. Remove from heat and stir in chocolate chips until melted. Cool to room temperature.

Hershey Foods Corporation   **Hershey Pennsylvania**

PUDDING CAKE

2 tablespoons shortening, melted
1 cup brown sugar, packed
¼ cup cocoa
wder
1¾ cups hot water
whipped cream or vanilla ice
cream for topping

Heat oven to ~~~ ~~grees. Measure flour, sugar, 2 tablespoons cocoa, baking powder, and salt into bowl. Blend in milk and shortening. Pour into ungreased 9" square pan. Stir together brown sugar and ¼ cup cocoa; sprinkle over batter. Pour hot water over batter. Bake for 45 minutes.

While hot, spoon onto dessert plate and top with whipped cream or a scoop of vanilla ice cream.

"One of my family's all-time favorites ... a perfect flavor combination."

Linda Paskins   **Cordova Sr. High School, Rancho Cordova**

COCOA FUDGE CAKE

Serves 6 to 8

1 cup flour
¾ cup sugar
⅓ cup cocoa
¾ teaspoon baking soda
¾ cup buttermilk

¼ cup shortening
1 egg
½ teaspoon vanilla
½ teaspoon salt

Mix all ingredients together in a large bowl. Beat on high for 2 minutes. Pour into a square 8" pan and bake at 350 degrees for 30 minutes.

"This is a wonderfully rich chocolate cake that needs no frosting. Serve with pie cherries on top."

Jeri Drake Lane   **Canyon Springs High School, Moreno Valley**

NAMELESS CAKE

Serves 12

¾ cup shortening
1½ cups sugar
3 eggs, well beaten
1¾ cups flour
½ teaspoon baking powder
½ teaspoon baking soda
½ teaspoon salt
¾ teaspoon nutmeg
1 teaspoon cinnamon
2 tablespoons cocoa

¾ cup sour milk
1 teaspoon vanilla
½ cup nuts
Frosting:
6 tablespoons butter
1 egg yolk
3 cups powdered sugar
1½ tablespoons cocoa
1 teaspoon cinnamon
1½ tablespoons hot coffee

Cream shortening; add sugar gradually. Cream thoroughly. Blend in well beaten eggs. Sift dry ingredients together and add to creamed mixture alternately with sour milk. Blend in vanilla and nuts. Pour into two 9" round cake pans. Bake at 350 degrees for 30 minutes. Cool.

Frosting: Cream butter; blend in egg yolk. Sift together dry ingredients and add to creamed mixture alternately with hot coffee. Beat until smooth. If necessary, add a few more drops of coffee until icing spreads easily.

"My mother always made this cake when I was a child. It was my favorite."

Linda Winzenread   **Whittier High School, Whittier**

EGGLESS COCKEYED CAKE

Serves 6

1½ cups flour
3 tablespoons cocoa
1 teaspoon soda
1 cup sugar
½ teaspoon salt
5 tablespoons cooking oil

1 tablespoon vinegar
1 teaspoon vanilla
1 cup cold water
½ cup nuts, chopped (optional)
½ cup chocolate chips (optional)
Cool Whip for topping

Sift flour, cocoa, salt, and soda together in a bowl. Mix in sugar. Add oil, vinegar, vanilla, and water, and mix. Beat by hand until nearly smooth. If desired, top with chocolate chips and nuts before baking (it is good even without these last two ingredients). Pour into 9" square greased pan and bake at 350 degrees for 30 minutes. Top with Cool Whip to serve.

"This cake is so good no one will ever know how easy it is to make. If you leave out the chips and nuts and use cholesterol-free oil, it is almost cholesterol free. Everything can be mixed directly in the pan if you wish."

Lura Staffanson   **Perris High School, Perris**

BANANA BAVARIAN TORTE

Serves 10

4 eggs, separated
1 cup sugar
1 cup graham cracker crumbs
½ teaspoon baking powder
½ cup walnuts, chopped
½ cup coconut, flaked
2 teaspoons vanilla

1 package instant vanilla
   pudding mix
1⅔ cups milk
2 bananas
¼ cup lemon juice
½ cup cream, whipped
¼ cup sugar

Beat egg yolks with sugar, cracker crumbs, baking powder, walnuts, coconut, and 1 teaspoon vanilla. In another bowl, beat egg whites till stiff peaks form. Fold into crumb mixture. Line two 8" layer pans with wax paper and place mixture into pans. Bake at 350 degrees for 20 to 25 minutes. Cool. Mix vanilla pudding with the milk; chill. Place first layer with pudding and slices of banana, sliced oriental style, and dipped in lemon juice. Place second layer and repeat with pudding. Whip cream and add sugar and 1 teaspoon vanilla. Place whipped cream and then bananas on top. Chill and serve.

Nancy Jordan   **Merced High School, Merced**

FAVORITE GINGERBREAD

Serves 9

½ cup shortening
2 tablespoons sugar
1 egg
1 cup dark molasses
1 cup boiling water

2¼ cups flour, sifted
1 teaspoon soda
½ teaspoon salt
1 teaspoon ginger
1 teaspoon cinnamon

Mix thoroughly the shortening, sugar, and egg. Blend in the molasses and water. Sift together the dry ingredients and stir into mixture, beating until smooth. Pour into well greased and floured 9" square pan. Bake at 325 degrees for 45 to 50 minutes.

"I serve whipping cream with the gingerbread."

Nancy Earnest   **Victor Valley High School, Victorville**

SURPRISE SOUR CREAM PUDDING CAKE

Serves 12

2 tablespoons butter	*⅛ teaspoon salt*
½ cup sugar	*1 cup milk*
1 teaspoon vanilla	*1 cup brown sugar*
1 egg, beaten	*1 cup sour cream*
1½ cups flour	*nuts (optional)*
2 teaspoons baking powder	*cream for serving*

Cream butter and sugar; add vanilla and egg. Add sifted dry ingredients alternately with milk. Beat thoroughly. Pour into a deep buttered 8" square pan. Sprinkle top with brown sugar and carefully spread sour cream over the brown sugar. Sprinkle nuts on top, if desired. Bake at 375 degrees for 30 to 40 minutes. Batter rises to the top, cream and sugar form a caramel sauce. Turn upside down immediately. Serve hot or cold with cream.

"This recipe is from my college days at Humboldt College, which were full of wonderful new experiences, as this recipe will be for you!"

Brenda Burke　　　　　　　　　　　**Mt. Whitney High School, Visalia**

POTATO CAKE

Serves 10 to 12

1 cup butter	*1 teaspoon cloves*
2 cups sugar	*1 teaspoon nutmeg*
1 cup hot potatoes, mashed	*1½ teaspoons cinnamon*
(not instant)	*5 tablespoons cocoa*
4 egg yolks, beaten	*½ cup milk*
2 cups flour, sifted	*1 cup walnuts, chopped*
½ teaspoon salt	*4 egg whites*
2 teaspoons baking powder	

Cream butter and sugar until fluffy. Add mashed potatoes and beaten egg yolks. Sift together flour, salt, baking powder, cloves, nutmeg, cinnamon, and cocoa; add alternately to cream mixture with milk. Add nuts. Beat egg whites until they form stiff peaks and fold into cake batter. Grease and flour two 8" square pans. Fill and bake at 350 degrees for 25 to 30 minutes. Frost with favorite frosting.

Simone Clements　　　　　　　.　　　**Bret Harte High School, Altaville**

WINE CAKE

Serves 10 to 12

1 package white or yellow cake
   mix
1 small package instant vanilla
   pudding
4 eggs

¾ cup vegetable oil
¾ cup cream sherry
1 teaspoon nutmeg
1 teaspoon almond extract

Mix all ingredients in the order listed. Beat on low for five minutes. Pour into well greased angel food cake pan and bake for 45 minutes at 350 degrees. After cake has cooled, sprinkle top with powdered sugar.

"A simple recipe, but a real crowd pleaser!"

Linda Woolley   **La Sierra High School, Riverside**

MOM'S AMARETTO CAKE

Makes one cake

1½ cups almonds, chopped
1 package (18½ oz.) yellow cake
mix without pudding
1 package (3½ oz.) vanilla
instant pudding
4 eggs
½ cup vegetable oil
½ cup water

½ cup amaretto liqueur
1 teaspoon almond extract
Glaze:
¼ cup water
½ cup sugar
2 tablespoons butter
¼ cup amaretto liqueur
½ teaspoon almond extract

Sprinkle 1 cup almonds in the bottom of a well greased tube pan. Combine next 7 ingredients. Beat on low speed; increase speed and beat 4 minutes. Stir in remaining ½ cup almonds. Pour batter in a tube pan and bake for 1 hour. Cool in pan for 15 minutes. Remove to cooling rack.

Glaze: Combine water, sugar, and butter in saucepan. Bring to a boil for 4 to 5 minutes until sugar dissolves. Cool 15 minutes. Stir in remaining ingredients. Poke holes in cake with wooden toothpick, pour glaze over cake.

"Use Baker's Joy (spray-on product to grease and flour pans) for fast, easy pan preparation. This cake is a real crowd pleaser."

Pam Amelotte   **Ocean View High School, Huntington Beach**

CHOCOLATE BUNDT CAKE

Makes one cake

1 package deep chocolate cake mix
1 package (4 oz.) instant chocolate pudding
½ pint sour cream
½ cup oil

½ cup warm water
4 eggs
1 package (12 oz.) chocolate chips
powdered sugar to sprinkle

Mix all ingredients, except powdered sugar, until well blended. Pour into well greased bundt pan. Bake at 350 degrees for 50 to 60 minutes. Cool in pan for 10 minutes, then turn out on serving plate. When thoroughly cooled, sprinkle with powdered sugar.

"A rich cake that all kids love! Great for chocoholics."

Linda Robinson　　　　　　　**Sinaloa Jr. High School, Simi Valley**

COFFEE CAKE SUPREME

Serves 12 to 16

1 white cake mix
1 large instant vanilla pudding
½ cup oil
4 eggs
1 carton (16 oz.) sour cream

¾ cup sugar
1 teaspoon cocoa powder
1 teaspoon cinnamon
1 cup walnuts, chopped

Preheat oven to 350 degrees. Grease and flour angel food cake pan. Mix cake mix, pudding, oil, eggs, and sour cream together. Beat well by hand till completely mixed. Set aside.

Mix sugar, cocoa, cinnamon, and walnuts together (sugar mixture). Pour half the cake mixture into prepared pan. Sprinkle with half the sugar mixture. Swirl batter with a knife. Repeat with remaining batter and sugar mixture. Bake at 350 degrees for 60 to 65 minutes.

"A favorite with family and friends."

Gail Lambert　　　　　　　**El Rancho Middle School, Anaheim**

MILKY WAY CAKE

Makes one cake

6 Milky Way bars
1 cup butter
2 cups sugar
4 large eggs
2½ cups flour, sifted
½ teaspoon baking soda
1¼ cups buttermilk

1 teaspoon vanilla
1 cup pecans, chopped
Frosting:
½ cup butter
3 Milky Way Bars
1½ cups powdered sugar, sifted
2 tablespoons milk

Melt together the 6 candy bars and ½ cup butter; set aside. Beat together ½ cup butter and sugar until fluffy. Add eggs, one at a time, to butter and sugar mixture; beat well. Add sifted flour and soda alternately with buttermilk to the sugar mixture, stirring until smooth. Add the melted candy, mixing well. Stir in vanilla and chopped nuts. Pour into greased and floured bundt pan. Bake at 350 degrees about 1 hour.

Milky Way Frosting: Melt together the butter and 3 candy bars. Stir in the sifted powdered sugar and milk. Drizzle over cake.

"The subtle taste of chocolate makes this a favorite with everyone."

Donna Collier   **John Muir Jr. High School, Burbank**

TRIPLE CHOCOLATE LUSCIOUS LAYER CAKE

Serves 10 to 12

1 package chocolate cake mix
1 package instant chocolate
   pudding mix
¾ cup oil
¾ cup milk
4 eggs

1 cup sour cream
1 package (12 oz.) chocolate
   chips
1 cup nuts, chopped
confectioners' sugar to sprinkle

Mix all ingredients together in a large bowl. Pour into greased bundt pan. Bake at 350 degrees for 50 to 60 minutes. Cool and sprinkle with confectioners' sugar.

"Super rich and super easy! Made all in one step."

Mary Springhorn   **Anderson Union High School, Anderson**

CHOCOLATE CHIP CAKE

Serves 10

4 eggs
¼ cup oil
1 small box vanilla instant
  pudding
½ cup sour cream

6 tablespoons cinnamon/sugar
  mixture
1 package (12 oz.) chocolate
  chips

Beat the first 4 ingredients. Pour half the batter into a greased bundt pan. Sprinkle with a cinnamon/sugar mixture and half package chocolate chips. Pour the rest of the batter in the pan and repeat with cinnamon/sugar and chocolate chips. Then marble it by running a knife through the batter. Add more cinnamon/sugar to top. Bake at 350 degrees for 1 hour.

"We've enjoyed this recipe for years."

Dorothy Wilson   **Dale Jr. High School, Anaheim**

HUMMINGBIRD CAKE

Serves 12

3 cups flour
2 cups sugar
1 teaspoon baking soda
1 teaspoon salt
1 teaspoon cinnamon
3 eggs, beaten
1½ cups oil
1½ teaspoons vanilla
1 can (8 oz.) pineapple, crushed

2 cups bananas, mashed
  (about 3)
1 cup walnuts, chopped
Frosting:
1 package (8 oz.) cream cheese
1 stick butter, softened
1 pound powdered sugar
1 teaspoon vanilla
1 cup walnuts, chopped

Grease and flour a 10" tube or bundt pan. Stir together the flour, sugar, baking soda, salt, and cinnamon in a large bowl. In a separate bowl, beat together eggs, oil, vanilla, pineapple, and banana. Add to flour mixture and mix well by hand. Stir in walnuts. Pour into prepared pan and bake at 350 degrees for 1 hour and 15 minutes. Cool on a rack for 15 minutes before removing from pan, then cool completely on rack. Cut cake into 2 layers and fill and frost cake.

Cream Cheese and Walnut Frosting: Cream cheese and butter together. Beat in the sugar until mixture is light and fluffy. Add vanilla. Fill and frost the cake. Sprinkle with chopped nuts.

"This cake gets its name because when you taste it, you go 'hummmmmm'!"

Marianne Estes   **La Mirada High School, La Mirada**

SANDTORTE

Serves 8 to 10

1 cup (2 cubes) butter
3 cups sugar
6 eggs
1 cup (½ pint) sour cream

3 cups flour
¼ teaspoon baking powder
1½ teaspoons vanilla
powdered sugar to sprinkle

Cream butter and then blend in sugar. Add eggs, one at a time, beating each time. Blend in sour cream. Sift flour and then sift again with baking powder. Add flour mixture in 4 to 5 parts to first mixture. Add vanilla and mix. Pour into well-buttered mold or tube pan. Bake at 350 degrees for 1½ hours or until it tests done with a toothpick. Cool 5 minutes in pan and turn onto cooling rack. Allow to cool completely and wrap in foil or plastic film and age 24 hours at room temperature before serving. Powdered sugar can be sprinkled on top if desired.

Dollie O'Banion   **Dos Palos High School, Dos Palos**

DARK, DELICIOUS FRUITCAKE

Makes one 10" tube or 2 9x5" loaf pans or 4 small loaf pans

3 cups flour
2 teaspoons baking powder
1 teaspoon salt
2 teaspoons cinnamon
½ teaspoon allspice
½ teaspoon ground cloves
½ teaspoon nutmeg
2 cups (1 lb.) mixed candied fruit
1 cup candied pineapple
1 cup whole candied cherries
1 cup candied citron (optional)

1 pound raisins
8 ounces pitted dates, cut into pieces
2 cups walnuts or pecans, halved
4 eggs
1¾ cups brown sugar, firmly packed
1 cup liquid (milk, water, or fruit juice)
¼ cup sorghum
¾ cup margarine, melted

Combine flour, baking powder, salt, cinnamon, allspice, cloves, and nutmeg in *large* bowl. Add candied fruit, pineapple, cherries, citron, raisins, dates, and nuts. Mix until all fruits and nuts are well coated with dry ingredients. In separate bowl, beat eggs until foamy. Gradually add brown sugar, beating until light and fluffy. Blend in liquid, sorghum, and melted margarine. Add to fruit mixture; stir until well blended. Pour batter into greased pans about ⅔ to ¾ full. Bake at 275 degrees for 2 to 2½ hours or until tester inserted into center comes out clean. Cool in pans about 30 minutes. Remove from pans; let cool completely. Wrap in foil to keep moist.

"This recipe has been 'perfected' over the years with help from my husband and son. It's one of their favorite holiday traditions."

Hazel G. Alexis   **Thompson Jr. High School, Bakersfield**

CRANBERRY COFFEE CAKE

Serves 10 to 12

½ cup butter, softened
1 cup sugar
2 eggs
2 cups flour
1 teaspoon baking powder
½ teaspoon salt
1 cup sour cream
1 teaspoon almond extract

½ cup walnuts, chopped
1 can (7 oz.) whole cranberry
   sauce
Glaze:
¾ cup powdered sugar
½ teaspoon almond extract
2 tablespoons hot water
½ cup walnuts, chopped

Cream together butter and sugar. Add eggs, one at a time. Sift together the flour, baking powder, and salt. Add sifted ingredients to batter, alternating with sour cream. Stir in almond extract and nuts. Pour half the batter into greased and floured bundt pan. With the back of a spoon, create a trough around center of batter. Carefully fill with cranberry sauce, so as not to reach sides. Top with remaining batter. Bake at 350 degrees for 50 to 60 minutes until cake springs back to touch. Cool on rack.

Glaze: Combine powdered sugar, almond extract, and hot water. Pour over cooled cake as a glaze. Top with walnuts.

"Great for breakfast or as a light dessert."

Jeri Lynn Stubblefield   **Lemoore High School, Lemoore**

POUND CAKE

Serves 12 to 20

1 pound butter
1 pound powdered sugar
6 eggs

3 cups cake flour
1 tablespoon vanilla extract
1 tablespoon lemon extract

Cream butter and sugar. Add 2 eggs; beat. Add 1 cup cake flour; beat. Repeat egg and cake flour additions two more times. Add extracts and beat for 5 minutes. Put into a greased and lightly floured bundt or tube cake pan. Bake at 350 degrees for 1 hour and 15 minutes, or until done.

"An old family recipe. Great for many things."

Inez Roberson   **Correia Jr. High School, San Diego**

7-UP POUND CAKE

Serves 8 to 10

3 cups sugar
1½ cups (3 sticks) margarine or
  butter
5 eggs

3 cups cake flour
¾ cup 7-Up
2 tablespoons lemon extract
powdered sugar for garnish

In a large bowl, beat sugar and margarine until light and fluffy with electric mixer. Add eggs and beat. Add in and beat the cake flour, a cup at a time. Add in and beat 7-Up and extract. Pour into a greased bundt pan. Bake at 325 degrees for 70 minutes. Garnish with sifted powdered sugar.

"Light with great lemon flavor. Can freeze for later use."

Bobbette Smith　　　　　　　　　　　　**Tokay High School, Lodi**

YOGURT POUND CAKE

Makes one 10" cake

½ cup butter or margarine
1½ cups sugar
3 eggs, separated
1 teaspoon vanilla

2 cups flour
½ teaspoon salt
½ teaspoon soda
1 cup plain yogurt

Beat together butter and 1 cup sugar until creamy. Beat in egg yolks and vanilla. Mix flour, salt, and soda. Stir into creamed mixture alternately with yogurt. Beat egg whites. Gradually add remaining ½ cup sugar. Continue beating until stiff peaks form. Fold into batter thoroughly. Turn into greased and floured 2-quart mold or 10" tube pan. Bake at 350 degrees for one hour. Cool for 10 minutes in pan, then invert onto wire rack to cool.

"Very moist cake, excellent with fresh fruit or whipped cream and chocolate curls."

Sue Waterbury　　　　**San Luis Obispo High School, San Luis Obispo**

FRESH APPLESAUCE CAKE

Serves 12

1½ cup sugar
1 cup vegetable oil
2 eggs
2 cups flour
½ teaspoon salt

1 teaspoon soda
1 teaspoon cinnamon
3 large pippin apples, peeled and
  sliced

Mix sugar and oil. Add eggs. Sift flour with salt, soda, and cinnamon. Mix in apples. You will be able to mix about half with your mixer, then you will need to mix by hand. Pour into oblong pan. Bake at 350 degrees for 1 hour.

Norma Koda　　　　**Katherine Edwards Intermediate School, Whittier**

OLD FASHIONED CHOCOLATE CAKE

Makes one cake

2 squares baking chocolate
1 cup boiling water
1 egg
¼ cup butter
1 cup sugar

1¼ cups flour
1½ teaspoons baking powder
1 scant teaspoon baking soda
1 teaspoon vanilla
½ teaspoon salt

Melt chocolate squares in ½ cup boiling water; mix well. Add egg, butter, sugar, flour, baking powder, baking soda; mix well. Add second ½ cup boiling water, vanilla, and salt. Bake at 350 degrees for 30 to 35 minutes for single 9 x 13" layer, or 20 to 25 minutes for 2 cake pans.

"This recipe comes from Great Aunt Flo. It's a wonderful, moist, old-fashioned cake!"

Robyn Nadell   **Bernardo Yorba Jr. High School, Yorba Linda**

CHOCOLATE APPLESAUCE CAKE

Serves 12 to 15

½ cup margarine, softened
1¾ cups sugar
2 eggs
2 cups applesauce
2 cups flour
3 tablespoons cocoa

1½ teaspoons baking soda
½ teaspoon salt
½ teaspoon cinnamon
1 cup chocolate chips
½ cup nuts, chopped
2 tablespoons sugar

In a large bowl, cream margarine and 1¾ cups sugar. Add eggs and applesauce. Mix well and set aside. Sift together flour, cocoa, soda, salt, and cinnamon. Add to large bowl and mix thoroughly. Pour into a greased and floured 13 x 9" pan. Sprinkle chocolate chips, nuts, and 2 tablespoons sugar on top. Bake at 350 degrees for 35 to 40 minutes.

"Great for picnics and sack lunches."

Linda Hsieh   **Rowland High School, Rowland Heights**

MISSISSIPPI MUD CAKE

Serves 20

2 cups sugar
1 cup shortening
4 eggs
1½ cups flour
⅓ cup cocoa
¼ teaspoon salt
3 teaspoons vanilla
1 cup pecans, chopped

½ bag miniature marshmallows
Frosting:
1 pound confectioners' sugar
1½ stick margarine, melted
½ cup evaporated milk
⅓ cup cocoa
1 teaspoon vanilla
1 cup pecans, chopped

Cream the sugar and shortening. Add eggs and beat. Sift together the flour, cocoa, and salt. Add to creamed mixture. Add vanilla and chopped nuts. Pour into greased 9 x 13" pan. Bake at 300 degrees for 30 minutes. Remove from oven and spread evenly with marshmallows. Return to oven and melt about 10 minutes.
Frosting: Sift sugar and cocoa together. Mix with margarine. Add evaporated milk, vanilla, and pecans. Spread on cake and let stand 2 hours or overnight.

"This has been in the family for many years. It keeps well and is great for traveling."

Margaret McLeod   **Nogales High School, La Puente**

WACKY CHOCOLATE CAKE

Makes one cake

3 cups flour
2 cups sugar
2 teaspoons baking soda
½ cup cocoa
1 teaspoon salt

1 cup salad oil
2 cups boiling water
2 teaspoons vanilla
2 teaspoons vinegar
few drops red food color

Mix together by hand the flour, sugar, baking soda, cocoa, and salt. Add remaining ingredients and mix well. Pour into a 9 x 13" pan, greased and floured. Bake at 350 degrees for 30 minutes.

"You don't need to frost this cake .. it's already great!"

Monica Carlson   **La Contenta Jr. High School, Yucca Valley**

COKE CAKE

Serves 12

2 cups sugar
2 cups flour, sifted
½ cup Crisco
½ cup butter
3 tablespoons cocoa
1 cup Coke Classic
½ teaspoon baking soda
½ cup buttermilk
2 eggs, beaten

1 teaspoon vanilla
1½ cups miniature
marshmallows
Frosting:
1 stick butter
6 tablespoons Coke Classic
3 tablespoons cocoa
1 pound powdered sugar
1 cup nuts, chopped

Mix sugar and flour in a bowl and set aside. Mix Crisco, butter, cocoa, and coke in a saucepan and bring to a rapid boil. Pour over dry ingredients and mix with a mixer. Dissolve the baking soda into the buttermilk and then add eggs, vanilla, and marshmallows. Mix and then and add to other mixture. Beat for 2 to 3 minutes (marshmallows won't completely dissolve). Pour into prepared 9 x 13" pan and bake at 350 degrees for 30 to 40 minutes.

Frosting: Bring butter, coke, and cocoa to a boil. When smooth, remove from heat and add powdered sugar and nuts. Beat until smooth. Pour over cake while frosting and cake are both hot.

"Serve a la mode and watch this cake disappear."

Linda Barnett   **Matilija Jr. High School, Ojai**

CHOCOLATE POTATO CAKE

2 cups sugar
¾ cup shortening
2 squares unsweetened chocolate, melted
1 cup potatoes, mashed
4 egg yolks
2 cups flour

½ teaspoon cinnamon
¼ teaspoon cloves
¼ teaspoon allspice
¼ teaspoon salt
1 cup buttermilk
1 teaspoon soda
4 egg whites, whipped

Blend sugar and shortening. Add melted chocolate, mashed potatoes, and egg yolks. Blend well. Sift together flour, spices, and salt. Add dry ingredients alternately with buttermilk (in which soda has been dissolved), starting and ending with flour. Fold in beaten egg whites. Pour into 9 x 13" baking pan. Bake at 300 degrees for 1 hour.

Naomi Wetzel   **Delta High School, Clarksburg**

DEEP CHOCOLATE UPSIDE DOWN CAKE

Makes 1 cake

½ cup butter (1 stick)
¼ cup water
1 cup brown sugar
1 cup walnuts, chopped

1⅓ cups flaked coconut
1 package Duncan Hines deep chocolate deluxe cake mix

Melt butter in a 13 x 9" baking dish. In a bowl, combine water and brown sugar, nuts and coconut. Mix well. Spread coconut mixture evenly in a baking dish over butter. Mix cake as directed on label, for 2 minutes at medium speed. Pour batter over mixture in the baking dish. Bake at 350 degrees for 40 minutes until cake springs back when touched lightly. Let stand 5 minutes so topping begins to set. Then turn upside down onto large platter.

"Serve with whipped cream, if desired."

Astrid Curfman　　　　　　　　**Rogers Jr. High School, Long Beach**

ALMOND JOY CAKE

Serves 15 to 20

1 chocolate cake mix with pudding
1 large can evaporated milk
2½ cups sugar
26 large marshmallows
1 package (14 oz.) coconut

½ cup margarine
1 package (12 oz.) chocolate chips
1 package (3½ oz.) almonds, slivered

Bake chocolate cake according to directions on the box in a 9 x 13" pan. Mix together 1 cup evaporated milk, 1 cup sugar, marshmallows, and coconut. Cook together until marshmallows are melted and then pour over the hot cake.

Melt margarine in a saucepan. Add remaining 1½ cups sugar and ½ cup evaporated milk. Bring to a boil; add chocolate chips. Stir until chips are melted and add almonds. Pour over the cake.

"If you like the candy bar, you will love the cake! Very rich ... serve small pieces."

Marianne Estes　　　　　　　　**La Mirada High School, La Mirada**

TURTLE CAKE

Serves 12

1 German chocolate super moist
  cake mix
3 eggs
oil
1 bag Kraft caramels

1 cup chocolate chips
1 cup pecans, chopped
2/3 cup evaporated milk
powdered sugar to sprinkle

Prepare cake mix as directed, using eggs and oil according to package directions. Pour half the mix into a greased and floured 9 x 13" pan. Bake at 350 degrees for 15 minutes. Melt caramels and evaporated milk over low flame, stirring constantly. Pour mixture over cake. Sprinkle chips and pecans on top. Pour remaining cake batter and bake for 15 to 20 minutes more. (Cake may seem undercooked when poked with toothpick, since the filling remains soft...no need to worry.) Let cool and sprinkle with powdered sugar.

"A very rich and filling dessert. A favorite of family and friends."

Katie Placido   **Warren High School, Downey**

BUTTERMILK FUDGE CAKE

Makes one cake

2 cups flour
2 cups sugar
1 stick margarine or butter
1/2 cup shortening
1 cup water
4 tablespoons cocoa
2 eggs, slightly beaten
1/2 cup buttermilk
1 teaspoon cinnamon
1 teaspoon salt

1 teaspoon baking soda
1 teaspoon vanilla
Icing:
1 cube margarine or butter
1/3 cup buttermilk
4 tablespoons cocoa
1 pound powdered sugar
1 teaspoon vanilla
1 cup nuts, chopped

Mix the flour and sugar; set aside. Melt together the margarine, shortening, water, and cocoa. Add the remaining ingredients and mix. Pour into greased and floured cookie sheet with 1" sides or an oblong pan. For cookie sheet, bake at 350 degrees for 20 minutes. For oblong pan, bake a little longer.

Icing: Five minutes before cake is done, start icing. Melt margarine in a saucepan; add buttermilk and cocoa and bring to boil. Remove from heat and add powdered sugar, vanilla, and nuts. Mix and spread over hot cake.

Donna Fippin   **Bret Harte High School, Altaville**

CHOCOLATE SHEET CAKE

Serves a crowd

8 tablespoons cocoa
1½ cups (3 sticks) margarine
1 cup water
2 cups sugar
2 cups flour
½ cup buttermilk

½ teaspoon soda
2 eggs
1 teaspoon vanilla
⅓ cup regular milk
1 box powdered sugar
1 cup nuts, chopped

Combine 4 tablespoons cocoa, 2 sticks margarine, and 1 cup water in a saucepan and bring to a boil. Pour over the sugar and flour. Then add the buttermilk, soda, eggs, and vanilla and mix well. Pour into a greased jelly roll pan. Bake at 400 degrees for 20 minutes.

Frosting: Melt 1 stick margarine, 4 tablespoons cocoa, and regular milk. Add the powdered sugar and nuts. Frost while cake is still warm.

Jennifer Formoe   **Temecula Valley High School, Temecula**

CHOCOLATE ANGEL ROLL

Makes 2 pans, serving 10 each

1 angel food cake mix
2 cups powdered sugar
2 cups milk
2 packages (4 oz. each)
  chocolate instant pudding mix
1 cup pecans, chopped

2 chocolate coated toffee candy
  bars, chopped
1 carton (8 oz.) Cool Whip,
  thawed
2 tablespoons chocolate-flavored
  syrup
10 each pecan halves

Heat oven to 350 degrees and prepare cake mix as directed on package, except spread half of the batter in each of 2 ungreased 15 x 10 x 1" jelly roll pans. Bake until light golden brown; cool 10 minutes. Loosen cakes from edges of pan and invert on towel; sprinkle with powdered sugar. Trim off stiff edge of cake while hot. Carefully roll each cake and towel from narrow end. Cool on wire rack. Beat milk and pudding until blended. Stir pecans and candy into pudding mixture. Reserve ¾ cup of whipped topping. Fold remaining topping into pudding mixture. Unroll one cake, remove towel, spread half pudding mixture over cake, roll up, sprinkle with powdered sugar; drizzle with chocolate syrup. Top with whipped topping and pecan halves. Refrigerate 1 hour.

"This cake can be frozen easily covered, up to 2 weeks. Before serving, cut into slices and let stand 20 minutes. An electric knife works best for cutting."

Linda Miley   **Quartz Hill High School, Quartz Hill**

MYSTERY PUDDING CAKE

Serves 10 to 12

1 cup flour
1 cup sugar
1 teaspoon salt
1 teaspoon baking soda
1 teaspoon cinnamon
1 egg, beaten
1 cup nuts, chopped
1 can (16 oz.) fruit cocktail, with
*   juice*

Topping:
1 small package instant vanilla
*   pudding*
½ pint whipping cream
1 teaspoon vanilla
2 tablespoons sugar

Preheat oven to 325 degrees. In a 7 x 11" or 9 x 13" baking dish, combine flour, sugar, salt, soda, and cinnamon. Stir in egg, nuts, and fruit cocktail. Bake 45 to 60 minutes till top springs back when touched and color is dark golden brown.
Topping: Combine pudding mix, whipping cream, vanilla, and sugar and blend well. Chill. Pour over individual servings.

"My grandmother used to make this, and it's always been one of my favorites."

Penny Niadna   **Golden West High School, Visalia**

FRESH APPLE CAKE

Serves 8 to 10

2 cups sugar
2 eggs
½ cup oil
2 cups flour
2 teaspoons baking soda
1 teaspoon salt

2 teaspoons cinnamon
1 teaspoon nutmeg
4 cups Granny Smith or Pippin
*   apples, peeled and chopped*
1 cup raisins
1 cup nuts, chopped

In large mixing bowl, combine sugar, eggs, and oil. Mix well. In a separate bowl, mix together the flour, baking soda, salt, cinnamon, and nutmeg. Add to first bowl (mixture will be a little stiff). Stir in apples, raisins, and nuts. Spread mixture into an oiled 9 x 13" baking pan. Bake at 350 degrees for 40 to 45 minutes.

"Great with vanilla ice cream. I make several for gifts at Christmas."

Julie Shelburne   **Tulare Union High School, Tulare**

CARROT CAKE

Serves 15

Cake:
2 cups flour
2 teaspoons baking soda
2 teaspoons cinnamon
½ teaspoon salt
3 eggs
¾ cup oil
¾ cup buttermilk
2 cups sugar
2 teaspoons vanilla
1 can (8 oz.) pineapple, crushed
and drained
2 cups carrots, grated
3½ oz. shredded coconut
1 cup walnuts, chopped

Glaze:
1 cup sugar
½ teaspoon baking soda
½ cup buttermilk
¼ pound butter or margarine
1 tablespoon corn syrup
1 teaspoon vanilla
Frosting:
¼ pound butter or margarine
1 package (8 oz.) cream cheese
1 teaspoon vanilla
2 cups powdered sugar
1 teaspoon orange juice
1 teaspoon orange peel, grated

Sift flour, baking soda, cinnamon, and salt together; set aside. In a large bowl, beat eggs. Add oil, buttermilk, sugar, and vanilla; mix well. Add flour mixture, pineapple, carrots, coconut, and walnuts; stir well. Pour into greased and floured 9 x 13" pan. Bake at 350 degrees for 55 minutes. Poke holes in hot cake with a wooden spoon handle and pour buttermilk glaze over hot cake. Cool cake before frosting.
Buttermilk Glaze: In small saucepan, mix sugar, soda, buttermilk, butter/margarine, and corn syrup; bring to a boil. Cook 5 minutes, stirring occasionally. Remove from heat and stir in vanilla.
Frosting: Cream butter/margarine and cream cheese until fluffy. Add vanilla, powdered sugar, orange juice, and orange peel until smooth.

"This is the best carrot cake I have ever tasted. The buttermilk glaze keeps it moist for several days."

Katie Morrison-Gold   **Olive Peirce Middle School, Ramona**

CARROT-PINEAPPLE CAKE

Serves 12

1½ cups flour
1 cup sugar
1 teaspoon baking powder
1 teaspoon baking soda
¼ teaspoon salt
⅔ cup oil
2 large eggs

1 cup carrots, shredded
½ cup pineapple, crushed with
 syrup
1 teaspoon vanilla
½ cup raisins (optional)
½ cup walnuts, chopped
 (optional)

Thoroughly combine flour, sugar, baking powder, soda, and salt. In another bowl, mix the oil, eggs, shredded carrot, crushed pineapple with syrup, and vanilla; then add to the dry ingredients and beat for 2 minutes. If desired, blend in raisins and nuts. Pour batter into a greased 9 x 13" pan. Bake at 350 degrees for about 50 minutes.

"Received acclaim from my foods classes and family, including my real gourmet son-in-law!"

Laurine Schneider   **Downey High School, Downey**

FRUIT COCKTAIL CAKE

Serves 12

1 can (16 oz.) fruit cocktail
2 cups flour
1½ cups sugar
2 eggs
2 teaspoons baking soda
⅛ teaspoon salt

⅔ cup brown sugar
½ cup walnuts, chopped
Sauce:
1 stick butter or margarine
1½ cups sugar
1 can (5 oz.) evaporated milk

Mix the fruit cocktail (including juice), flour, sugar, eggs, baking soda, and salt together in a mixing bowl. Mix by hand--do not use an electric mixer. Pour into a well greased 13 x 9" baking pan. Sprinkle the top of the cake with the brown sugar and chopped walnuts. Bake at 325 degrees for 45 minutes.
Sauce: While the cake is baking, bring the butter, sugar, and canned milk to a boil in a small saucepan. When the cake is done, use a fork to poke holes in it and pour the sauce on it. Cool before serving.

"A family favorite, given to us by a friend in Georgia. Always a hit at potlucks--moist and rich."

Stacy Sowell   **Juniper Intermediate School, Palmdale**

LEMON CAKE

Serves 8 to 12

1 box yellow cake mix
4 eggs
³⁄₄ cup water
³⁄₄ cup oil
1 small box lemon Jello

1 teaspoon lemon extract
½ cup butter, melted
1 cup powdered sugar
juice from 1 lemon

Mix together cake mix, eggs, water, oil, Jello, and lemon extract. Beat for 5 minutes. Pour into 9 x 13" baking pan and bake at 350 degrees for 25 to 30 minutes. Mix together butter, sugar, and juice. Poke holes in the cake, and pour mixture over cake, filling holes.

Reiko Ikkanda   **South Pasadena High School, South Pasadena**

MANDARIN ORANGE CAKE

Serves 10

1 cup sugar
1 cup flour
1 egg
1 teaspoon baking soda

1 can (11 oz.) mandarin oranges,
  with juice
½ teaspoon salt
1 teaspoon vanilla

Preheat oven to 350 degrees. Mix all ingredients in a blender and pour into a greased and floured 9 x 13" pan. Bake at 350 degrees for 30 to 40 minutes.

Glaze
³⁄₄ cup brown sugar

3 tablespoons butter
3 tablespoons milk

Bring all ingredients to a boil and pour over hot cake. Top with nuts or coconut and whipped cream, if desired.

"This moist cake is so easy and can be made quickly. It's one of our favorites."

Dorothy Wilson   **Dale Jr. High School, Anaheim**

PUMPKIN UPSIDE DOWN CAKE

Serves 12 or more

1 can (20 oz.) pumpkin
1¼ cups sugar
2 teaspoons cinnamon
½ teaspoon ginger
1 can (13 oz.) evaporated milk
3 eggs, beaten

1 teaspoon nutmeg
1 package yellow cake mix, with
  pudding
1 cup nuts, chopped
1½ cups butter

Mix first 7 ingredients together. Place mixture into a buttered 9 x 13" pan. Sprinkle yellow cake mix over pumpkin mixture; then sprinkle nuts. Drizzle 1½ to 2 cups butter on top and bake at 350 degrees for 1 hour.

"Delicious, not too filling."

Ginny Clark   **Sonora High School, La Habra**

PRUNE CAKE

1 cup sugar
3/4 cup oil
2 eggs
2 cups flour
2 tablespoons cocoa
1 teaspoon cinnamon
1/2 teaspoon nutmeg

1 1/2 teaspoons baking soda
1/2 teaspoon salt
1 cup evaporated milk,
   undiluted
1 cup prunes, cooked and
   chopped
1 cup nuts, coarsely chopped

Cream together the sugar and oil. Add eggs one at a time. Mix well. Sift together the flour, cocoa, cinnamon, nutmeg, baking soda, and salt. Gradually add the flour mixture to the creamed mixture, alternately with the evaporated milk. Add the prunes and nuts and mix well. Pour into a greased and floured 9 x 13" pan. Bake at 350 degrees for 35 to 40 minutes. Frost with any white frosting.

"Thin cake is moist and spicy with just a hint of chocolate. Makes good cupcakes, too!"

Gloria Walker   **Casa Roble Fundamental High School, Orangevale**

ZUCCHINI CAKE

Serves 15 to 20

2 cups flour
2 teaspoons baking soda
1 teaspoon salt
2 teaspoons cinnamon
1 1/2 cups sugar
1 1/4 cups vegetable oil
4 eggs

2 cups zucchini, grated
1/2 cup nuts, chopped
Frosting:
1/2 cup margarine or butter
1 package (8 oz.) cream cheese
1 teaspoon vanilla
1 pound powdered sugar

Mix all cake ingredients together. Bake in a 9 x 13" pan at 350 degrees for 35 to 40 minutes.

Cream Cheese Frosting: Cream together the margarine/butter, cream cheese, and vanilla; add the powdered sugar. (For less calories, instead of frosting, while cake is still warm, dust with powdered sugar.)

"A spicy, moist cake. Hard to tell it has zucchini in it!"

Jean Dempsey   **Santa Paula High School, Santa Paula**

PINEAPPLE CAKE

Serves 12

*1 can (20 oz.) pineapple, crushed
  with juice*
2 cups sugar
2 cups flour
2 teaspoons baking soda
*2 eggs and enough water to make
  ½ cup*

1 teaspoon vanilla
*1 package (8 oz.) cream cheese,
  softened*
1 stick butter, softened
2 cups powdered sugar

Mix first 6 ingredients together. Pour into a greased 9 x 13" pan. Bake at 350 degrees for 25 to 30 minutes.
Icing: Combine the cream cheese, butter, and powdered sugar; mix well. Spread on cake while it's still hot.

"This recipe was given to me by a math teaching friend in Lewisville, Texas. She got it from her mother, a home economics teacher. Delicious!"

Judy Banks   **Temecula Valley High School, Temecula**

DUMP CAKE

Serves 10 to 12

1 can (18 oz.) pineapple, crushed
1 can (18 oz.) cherry pie filling

1 box yellow cake mix
1 cube butter

Pour crushed pineapple into 9 x 13" ungreased cake pan; smooth out. Pour cherry pie filling over pineapple; smooth out. Put unmixed dry cake mix on top of cherry pie filling. Cut butter into pats and spread evenly over cake mix. Bake at 375 degrees for 30 to 45 minutes.
'cl"Very easy and quick to make ... and very good."

Nancy Bohte   **South Pasadena High School, South Pasadena**

PINEAPPLE-APPLE CAKE DESSERT

Serves 12

*1 can (20 oz.) pineapple, crushed
  with juice*
*1 can Comstock sliced apples
  (not apple pie filling)*
*1 lemon cake mix (without
  pudding)*

1 cup margarine, melted
1 cup coconut, shredded
1 cup walnuts, chopped

Layer pineapples, apples, and cake mix in a 9 x 13" pan. Drizzle with melted margarine. Top with coconut and walnuts. Bake at 350 degrees for 55 to 60 minutes.

Michelle Smith   **Kraemer Jr. High School, Placentia**

Chocoberry Mousse Cake, Page 32
Chocolate Almond Terrine with Raspberry Sauce, Page 104

Chocolate Praline Layer Cake, Page 2

Old Fashioned Praline Pecan Rolls, Page 150

Heavenly No-Bake Cheesecake, Page 47

PUMPKIN CAKE

Serves 6 to 8

2 cups cake flour, sifted
½ teaspoon salt
2 teaspoons cinnamon
1½ teaspoons soda
2 teaspoons baking powder
2 cups sugar
1 cup corn oil

4 eggs
2 cups canned pumpkin
Icing:
1 package (8 oz.) cream cheese
1 stick margarine, softened
1 box confectioners' sugar
1 teaspoon vanilla

Combine all ingredients for the cake in the order listed. Bake at 300 degrees for 1 hour. Cool and spread with the icing.
Icing: Mix all ingredients with mixer.

Olga Sarouhan   **Edison High School, Huntington Beach**

WALNUT CAKE

Serves 10

2 cups flour
2 cups sugar
2 eggs

2 teaspoons soda
1 cup walnuts, chopped
1 can (8 oz.) pineapple, crushed

Place first 4 ingredients in mixing bowl; blend together. Add walnuts and pineapple; mix until blended. Place in a 9 x 13'' greased pan. Bake at 350 degrees for 30 to 35 minutes. If desired, frost with a butter cream icing.

"A quick cake to take on a picnic with or without icing. Keeps moist!"

Maridel Anagnos   **Tokay High School, Lodi**

PUMPKIN BARS CAKE

Serves 12

1 large can pumpkin
1 cup brown sugar
4 teaspoons pumpkin pie spice
3 eggs

1 large can evaporated milk
1 package yellow cake mix
¼ cup margarine, melted
½ cup nuts, chopped

Blend together pumpkin, sugar, spice, eggs, and milk. Pour into 9 x 13'' baking dish. Crumble and sprinkle cake mix over pumpkin mixture. Drizzle margarine over top and then sprinkle with nuts. Bake at 350 degrees for 50 minutes.

"This is a bar cookie type dessert that makes a quick and easy alternative for traditional pumpkin pie."

Peg Della Zoppa   **Yucca Valley High School, Yucca Valley**

CHOCOLATE MOUSSE DESSERT CAKE

Serves 8 to 10

1 tablespoon instant coffee
4 tablespoons hot water
4 tablespoons dark Jamaican
rum
14 ounces semisweet baking
chocolate
2 ounces unsweetened baking
chocolate

6 large eggs
½ cup sugar
1 cup whipping cream, chilled
1 tablespoon pure vanilla extract
confectioners' sugar

Preheat oven to 350 degrees and place rack in lower third level. Prepare a 10-cup cake pan, preferably with nonstick lining, buttered, bottom lined with buttered wax paper, and floured. Use a roasting pan large enough to hold cake pan easily, fill with enough hot water to come halfway up cake pan, and set in oven. In a medium size saucepan, swirl the coffee and hot water; add the rum and break up the chocolate into the pan. Bring 2" of water to boil in a larger pan; remove from heat, and set chocolate pan in it; cover and let the chocolate melt while you continue with the recipe.

Break the eggs into a bowl; add the sugar and stir over hot water for several minutes until eggs are slightly warm to your finger. Then beat for 5 minutes or more, until mixture has at least tripled in volume and forms a thick ribbon when a bit is lifted and falls from the beater; the eggs should be the consistency of lightly whipped cream.

Pour cream into a metal mixing bowl. Empty a tray of ice cubes into a larger bowl; cover them with cold water, then set the cream bowl into the larger ice-filled bowl. Beat until cream has doubled in volume and holds its shape softly. Whip in the vanilla.

Beat the melted chocolate with a whisk; it should be smooth and silky. Scrape it into the egg/sugar mixture, blending rapidly with a rubber spatula, and when partially incorporated, fold in the whipped cream, deflating cream and eggs as little as possible. Turn batter into prepared cake pan, which will be about ⅔ full. Set it at once in the pan of hot water in the preheated oven. Cake will rise about ⅛" above edge of pan, and is done when a skewer or straw comes out clean after about 1 hour of baking. Then turn off oven, leave door ajar, and let cake sit for 30 minutes in its pan of water, so that it will sink evenly. Remove from oven, still in its pan of water, and let sit for another 30 minutes so it will firm up before unmolding. Cake will sink down as it cools to about its original volume. Unmold cake and decorate with a sprinkling of confectioners' sugar.

"Cake is most tender when eaten slightly warm."

Pat Wong   **Taft High School, Taft**

ULTIMATE MOCHA DESSERT

Serves 12 to 14

Crust
1 cup flour
1/4 cup dark brown sugar
1/4 cup cocoa
3/4 cup pecans, finely chopped
1/2 cup butter
1/4 teaspoon salt
1 teaspoon vanilla
2 tablespoons water

Filling
3/4 cup butter
1 cup dark brown sugar
1 tablespoon instant coffee powder
6 tablespoons cocoa
3 eggs

Topping
1 1/2 cups heavy whipping cream
1/3 cup powdered sugar
4 teaspoons instant coffee powder

Garnish
1/2 cup heavy whipping cream
2 tablespoons powdered sugar
1 teaspoon vanilla
1/4 cup coating chocolate, melted

Crust: In a medium bowl, combine flour, brown sugar, cocoa, pecans, butter, and salt. When well mixed, sprinkle with vanilla and water and stir with a fork until well blended. Press into a 10" springform pan until an even layer is formed. Bake at 350 degrees for 20 minutes. Cool on a wire rack.

Filling: In a large bowl, beat butter until fluffy. Add brown sugar and beat until light and fluffy. Beat in coffee powder and cocoa. Add eggs, one at a time, beating well after each addition. Spread batter evenly over the baked and cooled crust. Cover and chill several hours or overnight.

Topping: About 1 hour before serving, combine heavy cream, powdered sugar, and instant coffee powder in a medium bowl; beat until very stiff. Loosen edges of dessert with a sharp knife and remove sides of pan. Place on serving plate and spread evenly with the whipped cream topping. Refrigerate.

Garnish: In a small bowl, whip cream, powdered sugar, and vanilla until stiff. Put into a decorating bag with a star point tip. Make individual shells on each serving piece, starting at the outside and ending about halfway to the center. With a fork, drizzle melted chocolate over each shell.

Refrigerate until serving time.

"This dessert also freezes very well."

Nancy Bruce   **San Juan High School, Citrus Heights**

CHOCOBERRY MOUSSE CAKE

Serves 12

1 9" yellow or white cake layer
2 pints fresh strawberries, tops
  removed
1 envelope unflavored gelatin
1²/₃ cups milk, divided
²/₃ cup sugar
½ cup unsweetened cocoa

2 tablespoons butter or
  margarine
¾ teaspoon vanilla
2 egg whites
1 tablespoon sugar
½ cup whipping cream, chilled

Remove bottom from 9" springform pan. Line sides of pan with plastic wrap extending wrap over top edge; put bottom back in place over wrap. Place cake layer in pan. Halve about 10 strawberries; place cut side out around edge of cake (between cake and pan). Chill while preparing top layer.

In medium saucepan, sprinkle gelatin over 1 cup milk; let stand several minutes to soften. Combine ²/₃ cup sugar and cocoa; add to mixture in saucepan. Cook over low heat, stirring constantly, until mixture boils. Remove from heat; stir in butter until melted. Blend in remaining ²/₃ cup milk and vanilla. Cool; chill until mixture begins to set, stirring occasionally.

Beat egg whites with 1 tablespoon sugar until stiff peaks form; carefully fold into chocolate mixture. Beat whipping cream until stiff; gently fold into chocolate mixture. Pour over cake in pan; chill several hours or until set. To serve, halve and sweeten remaining strawberries. Serve over wedges of dessert.

Hershey Foods Corporation   **Hershey, Pennsylvania**

CHOCOLATE LAYERED DESSERT

½ cup margarine
1 cup flour
½ cup nuts, chopped
1 package (8 oz.) cream cheese
1 cup powdered sugar
2 cartons (8 oz.) Cool Whip

1 package (6 oz.) instant
  chocolate pudding
2½ cups milk
chopped nuts or chocolate
  shavings, for garnish

1st Layer: Cut margarine into flour until mixture is crumbly. Stir in nuts. Pat into bottom of ungreased 9 x 13" pan. Bake at 350 degrees for 10 to 12 minutes. Cool.

2nd Layer: Cream together the cream cheese and powdered sugar. Stir in 1 carton Cool Whip. Spread mixture over cooled crust.

3rd Layer: Mix the pudding mix and milk (it will be pretty thick). Spread over second layer.

4th Layer: Spread 1 carton Cool Whip over third layer. Sprinkle with chopped nuts or chocolate shavings for garnish. Refrigerate.

"May be made a day ahead. Recipe can be cut in half and made in one 8" square pan. Decorate top for special occasions, such as birthdays, Valentine's Day, etc."

Jan Ehrenberg   **Badger Springs School, Moreno Valley**

HEAVENLY DELIGHT

Makes one cake

1 large pudding (any flavor)
1 ngel food cake (store bought or
your own)

1 container (8 oz.) Cool Whip
2 Heath candy bars

Make pudding according to package directions. Use a 9 x 13" pan, either glass or aluminum. Break up one half the cake in pieces, covering the bottom of the pan. Cover with the pudding. Top with remaining cake, broken into pieces. Cover with Cool Whip. Break up candy bars into pieces and sprinkle on top.

"Super easy to make. Takes 5 minutes."

Barbara Bressler   **Buena Park High School, Buena Park**

CHERRY BERRY ON A CLOUD

Serves 12 to 20

6 egg whites
½ teaspoon tartar
¼ teaspoon salt
1¾ cups sugar
3 packages (3 oz. each) cream
cheese
¾ cup sugar
1 teaspoon vanilla
pinch of salt

2 cups miniature marshmallows
2 cartons whipping cream,
whipped (do not use Cool
Whip)
1 can cherry pie filling
1 tablespoon lemon juice
1 package frozen raspberries
with juice

Beat egg whites, tartar, and salt together (like for a meringue). Add 1¾ cups sugar and beat. Heat oven to 270 degrees. Grease 9 x 13" pan. Put mixture into pan and bake for 60 minutes. Shut off oven and leave in overnight. Cream the cream cheese, ¾ cup sugar, vanilla, and a pinch of salt. Stir in the marshmallows and fold in pre-whipped cream. Spread over the meringue. At serving time, cut into squares and put on the topping.

Topping: Mix together cherry pie filling, lemon juice, and frozen raspberries.

"Absolutely melts in your mouth!! A wonderful dessert to serve to a group. Very light tasting. I have always received rave reviews for this."

Robin Nichols   **Clovis West High School, Fresno**

FAST 'N EASY CHOCOLATE DELIGHT

Serves 10

*1 package devils food cake mix
(plus eggs, oil and water
according to directions)
1 large Cool Whip*

*1 large package instant chocolate
pudding mix
3 cups milk (for pudding)
walnuts or Heath bars, chopped*

Mix devils food cake according to package directions. Bake in a 9 x 13" pan; cool. Mix pudding according to directions. Cut off edges of cake and discard. Cut the remaining cake into squares. Layer half the cake in a large bowl. Pour half the pudding on top, then half the Cool Whip. Sprinkle with chopped nuts or Heath bars. Repeat layers. Chill.

"I sometimes substitute ½ cup Kahlua and reduce the milk by ½ cup for the pudding ... yummy."

Gail Brunell   **Leuzinger High School, Lawndale**

AABLE KAGE (DANISH APPLE CAKE)

Serves 4 to 6

*2 cups bread crumbs
sugar and cinnamon to taste
2½ cups applesauce*

*1 pint whipping cream, whipped
red jelly to decorate*

Place ¼ of crumbs in a buttered 9" square pan or glass bowl. Layer crumbs, then sugar/cinnamon sprinkle, then applesauce, and repeat till all are used up. Allow to be refrigerated at least 2 hours or overnight. Serve chilled with whipped cream and decorate with 1 dab of red jelly on top!

"This special Danish recipe has been in my family before 1890 and I know it will be our favorite past the 1990s. Both Nana Rasmussen and Nana Taylor have served this recipe at Christmas and birthdays."

Shirley Blough   **Hillside Jr. High School, Simi Valley**

Candies
Candies
Candies

"SEE'S FUDGE" (ALMOST!)

Makes 64 servings

¾ cup evaporated milk
10 marshmallows
2 cups sugar
½ cup butter

1 cup (6 oz.) chocolate chips
1 cup walnuts or pecans, broken
  pieces
1 teaspoon vanilla

Put evaporated milk, marshmallows, and sugar in 3-quart saucepan and bring to a boil over medium heat, stirring constantly. Cook 6 minutes using timer. Remove pan from fire and add all of the other ingredients and stir well until butter and chips are thoroughly melted. Pour into buttered 8" square pan. Refrigerate (tastes creamier if allowed to stand in refrigerator 2 days or longer).

"I've used this recipe in class over 30 years because it is almost foolproof. The story goes that a woman asked See's Candy Co. for their recipe, which they sent, along with a $5,000 invoice. She then made copies for all her acquaintances."

Carole Jackson   **Apple Valley High School, Apple Valley**

EASY FUDGE

2 packages chocolate chips
80 small marshmallows
1 teaspoon salt
1 cup (2 cubes) margarine

4½ cups sugar
1 can evaporated milk
1 tablespoon vanilla
⅔ cup walnuts

Put chocolate chips, marshmallows, and salt in a large bowl. Put margarine, sugar, and milk into an iron skillet or heavy pan and bring to a boil. Boil a full 5 minutes, stirring constantly. Pour over the chocolate chips and marshmallows. Add vanilla and nuts. Pour onto a buttered cookie sheet. Cool and cut into squares.

"This easy fudge is almost foolproof. Just be sure to boil it a full 5 minutes."

Lura Staffanson   **Perris High School, Perris**

PISTACHIO LEMON FUDGE

Makes about 4 to 5 dozen

*1 pound white chocolate,
  chopped
1 cup powdered sugar, sifted
½ cup corn syrup
¼ cup butter or margarine*

*1 cup unsalted pistachio nuts,
  chopped
1 tablespoon whipping cream
1 tablespoon lemon juice
1 teaspoon vanilla*

Combine first 4 ingredients in a 2-quart casserole (do not stir). Microwave at high for 3 minutes stirring once half way through. Beat until chocolate melts and mixture is smooth. Add pistachios, whipping cream, lemon juice, and vanilla, stirring until smooth. Pour mixture into a buttered 13 x 9" pan spreading with a spatula to form an even layer. Chill and cut into 1½" squares.

"Vanilla chips can be used in place of the white chocolate. This is a real gourmet treat!"

Sue Hope   **Lompoc High School, Lompoc**

MILLIONAIRE FUDGE

Yields 1 cookie sheet full

*4 cups sugar
1 can evaporated milk
½ cup margarine
24 ounces chocolate almond bars*

*12 ounces chocolate chips
1 pint marshmallow creme
1 tablespoon vanilla
2 cups nuts, chopped (optional)*

Mix together sugar, milk, and margarine in a saucepan. Boil for 10 minutes, stirring constantly. Remove from heat and add chocolate bars, chocolate chips, marshmallow creme, vanilla, and nuts. Stir until all ingredients are dissolved and mixed well. Pour onto a well greased cookie sheet. Let stand 12 hours or overnight.

"I don't like fudge, but this is terrific!"

Monica Carlson   **La Contenta Jr. High School, Yucca Valley**

NO-COOK FUDGE

Makes 3 dozen

*½ cup butter or margarine
⅓ cup boiling water
4½ cups powdered sugar, sifted
½ cup nonfat dry milk powder*

*½ cup unsweetened cocoa
  powder
dash of salt*

Stir butter into boiling water. Stir till melted. Beat in sugar, nonfat dry milk powder, cocoa, and salt. Pour into buttered 8" square baking pan. Refrigerate several hours and cut into squares.

Kathie Baczynski   **Mt. Carmel High School, San Diego**

COCONUT MOUNDS BARS

Makes about 80

2 pounds confectioners' sugar
1 can (14 oz.) sweetened
 condensed milk
1 cup nuts, chopped
1 package (14 oz.) coconut

1 cup (2 sticks) butter or
 margarine, softened
3 packages (6 oz. each) milk
 chocolate chips
½ block paraffin wax (comes
 4 blocks to a box)

Mix sugar, condensed milk, nuts, coconut, and butter and mix thoroughly. Shape mixture into small balls about 1" diameter. Chill for 30 minutes. Melt chocolate and paraffin in a double boiler. Using a toothpick, dip each ball into chocolate mixture. Cool on waxed paper. Spoon chocolate into holes left by toothpicks.

"My home economics teacher gave me this recipe 20 years ago. I saved it and now pass it on to my students because it is so-o-o good."

Tanya Goosev   **Reedley High School, Reedley**

PEANUT BUTTER BONBONS

Makes 100

2 cups peanut butter
½ cup butter or margarine
4½ cups powdered sugar, sifted
3 cups crisp rice cereal

1 cup (6 oz.) butterscotch pieces
1 cup (6 oz.) semisweet
chocolate pieces

Melt peanut butter and butter. Mix sugar and rice cereal. Pour butter mixture over cereal mixture. Blend together with hands. Form into ½" balls. Chill till firm. Melt butterscotch pieces in top of double boiler over boiling water. Dip half the candies in coating; swirl tops. Place on waxed paper-lined baking sheet. Chill till firm. Repeat melting and dipping process with chocolate pieces and remaining candies. Chill till firm.

Kathie Baczynski   **Mt. Carmel High School, San Diego**

RUM BALLS

Makes about 4 dozen

32 vanilla wafers
1 cup pecans, chopped
2 tablespoons cocoa

4 tablespoons white corn syrup
4 tablespoons rum
confectioners' sugar

Crush wafers (or use a food processor) to make crumbs. Put into 1-quart mixer bowl. Blend in chopped nuts. Add cocoa, syrup, and rum and mix thoroughly. Coat hands with confectioners' sugar and roll mixture into ½" balls. Refrigerate for about 1 hour and then roll in confectioners' sugar.

"May substitute chocolate wafers."

Judi Topp   **Alder Jr. High School, Fontana**

CHOCOLATE CHEWS

Makes 3 dozen

½ cup shortening
1⅔ cups sugar
2 teaspoons vanilla
2 eggs
1 square (2 oz.) chocolate
2 cups flour, sifted

2 teaspoons baking powder
½ teaspoon salt
⅓ cup milk
½ cup walnuts
½ cup confectioners' sugar

Cream the shortening, sugar, and vanilla together. Beat eggs; add chocolate and beat well. Stir into shortening mixture. Sift dry ingredients together; add alternately with milk; blend well after each addition. Stir in nuts. Chill 2 to 3 hours and form into 1" balls. Roll in confectioners' sugar. Place on greased baking sheet 2 to 3 inches apart. Bake at 350 degrees about 20 minutes.

"This was a recipe found in my grandmother's file upon her death."

Mary Ann Christy   **Apple Valley High School, Apple Valley**

CHOCOLATE TRUFFLES

Makes 7 dozen

1 cup semisweet chocolate chips
1½ cubes margarine or butter
1 egg yolk
1¼ cups powdered sugar

1 tablespoon rum
1 tablespoon instant coffee
1 cup fine coconut or chocolate
 cookie crumbs

Melt chips over hot water and cool. Cream margarine, blend in egg yolk and sugar. Add rum, coffee, and chocolate. Mix well. Chill at least 1 hour till firm enough to handle. Drop ½" chunks into coconut and form into balls. Chill at least ½ hour on a cookie sheet to firm (or freeze). Keep in covered container in refrigerator or freezer.

Cheryl Pullan   **Terrace Hills Jr. High School, Grand Terrace**

TRUFFLES

Makes 8 to 12

1 cup heavy cream
2 tablespoons unsalted butter
1 pound semisweet chocolate bits
¾ tablespoon dark rum or Grand
 Marnier

½ pound semisweet chocolate
 bits
sprinkle choices (unsweetened
 cocoa powder, coconut, nuts)

Heat cream to boil. Remove from heat and add butter and chocolate bits. Stir with whisk until melted; add liqueur. Chill in freezer 3 to 4 hours. With melon baller, scoop out balls, roll in hand, and coat with melted chocolate bits. Sprinkle with your choice of topping. Place on wax paper and keep chilled until served.

"A rich treat after a meal, or when a simple get together needs bite-size sweets."

Jeanne Koerner   **Temecula Valley High School, Temecula**

CARAMEL TURTLES

1 pound caramels
3 tablespoons evaporated milk
2 tablespoons butter or
  margarine

1½ cups pecans (or walnuts)
1 package chocolate chips
½ bar paraffin

Heat caramels and milk in top of double boiler over lot heat. Stir until melted and creamy. Add margarine and nuts and mix. Drop by teaspoonfuls onto well-greased wax paper. Chill. Melt chocolate and wax over boiler. Take from heat and dip caramels to coat. Let dry and store until ready to serve.

"This recipe is compliments of my mother who serves them to her bridge club during the holidays. They taste just like the wonderful Sees candy version."

Robin Nichols   **Clovis West High School, Fresno**

CARAMELS

Makes 48 plus pieces

4 cups sugar
4 cups light corn syrup
½ pound butter
4 cups evaporated milk

6 cups walnuts
1 teaspoon vanilla
¼ teaspoon salt

In a heavy pot cook together sugar, corn syrup, and butter until 245 degrees on a medium heat. Do not remove from heat and gradually add the 4 cups of evaporated milk. Do not allow mixture to stop boiling at anytime. Cook at high heat, stirring constantly until mixture returns to 242 degrees. Remove from heat and add 6 cups of nuts (do not chop). Add vanilla and salt. Mix and turn into a buttered pan. Allow to cool and cut into squares. Wrap individually in plastic wrap.

"This is a good-lasting quality recipe ... caramels last for a year or more if stored well. Given to me by a college friend from Tennessee."

Darlene Lupul   **Tokay High School, Lodi**

BITTERSWEET CHOCOLATE CARAMELS WITH BURNT ALMONDS

Makes about 6 to 7 dozen

1½ cups sugar
¾ cup light corn syrup
¼ cup unsalted butter, cut into small pieces
2 tablespoons cold water
1 tablespoon amaretto liqueur
3 ounces unsweetened chocolate, melted

1 cup whipping cream, scalded and hot
10 ounces whole, unblanched almonds, toasted
2 teaspoons vanilla
¼ teaspoon salt

Lightly butter 11 x 15" nonstick baking sheet. Cook sugar, corn syrup, butter, water, and liqueur in heavy saucepan over low heat until sugar dissolves, swirling pan occasionally. Bring to a boil. Reduce heat to medium low. Stir in melted chocolate and simmer gently until candy thermometer registers 234 to 240 degrees (soft ball stage). Gradually stir in cream and cook, stirring constantly until candy thermometer registers 244 to 248 degrees (firm ball stage). Remove from heat. Chop almonds into 2 to 3 pieces each. Stir in almonds, vanilla, and salt. Pour caramel onto prepared sheet, tilting to cover sheet completely. Let cool about 15 minutes. Using a heavy knife, cut chocolate caramels lengthwise into strips. Using hands, form each strip into a roll. Cut each roll into pieces. Wrap in 4 x 6" pieces of wax paper. Roll tightly and twist ends. Store in airtight container. Best if enjoyed within ten days of preparation, but will keep up to one month in an airtight container.

"Wonderful. Great flavor!"

Gloria Reece   **Porterville High School, Porterville**

TRIPLE CHOCOLATE KISSES

Makes 24 individual kisses

2 egg whites
¼ teaspoon cream of tartar
¼ teaspoon almond extract
½ cup sugar

1 square (1 ounce) semisweet chocolate, grated
24 milk chocolate kisses
unsweetened cocoa powder

Beat egg white, cream of tartar, and almond extract in small bowl on medium speed till stiff peaks form (tips curl). Add sugar, slowly beating on high speed till stiff peaks form (tips stand straight up). Fold in grated chocolate. Spoon meringue into a decorating bag fitted with a star tip. On a lightly greased cookie sheet, pipe 24 rounds of meringue 1¼ inches in diameter. Lightly press a kiss into each meringue round. Pipe meringue around each kiss in concentric circles, starting at base and working toward top. **Cover kiss completely**. Dust with cocoa power. Bake at 325 degrees for 20 to 25 minutes or till lightly removable from cookie sheet. Cool immediately on wire rack.

"My students love them. They don't believe they don't melt all over the oven. I demonstrate them on Valentines Day. Only 44 calories each."

Deanne Moody   **Monte Vista High School, Spring Valley**

CHOCOLATE COVERED MARSHMALLOWS

Makes 48 to 50

1 cup chocolate chips
¼ cup shortening
2 cups nuts, chopped

chocolate sprinkles
1 package large marshmallows
50 wooden toothpicks

Place chocolate chips and shortening in glass measuring cup. Microwave for 1½ to 3 minutes or until chips are shiny and soft; then stir until smooth. Place nuts or candy sprinkles on shallow plate. Insert toothpick in top of each marshmallow. Dip marshmallow in chocolate to cover completely. Roll in nuts or sprinkles about ¾ of the way up the sides. Set on wax paper and let set until firm. Repeat until all have been dipped.

"We make these in class, wrapped in plastic wrap and tied with colorful yarn. They are a big hit!"

Libby Newman   **West Valley High School, Hemet**

HO-HO'S!!

Makes 50

1 cup chocolate chips
¼ cup shortening
2 cups nuts, chopped

50 small candy canes
1 package (10 oz.) large
marshmallows

Place chocolate chips and shortening in a 2-cup measure. Microwave at 50% power for 1½ to 3½ minutes, or until chips are shiny and soft. Stir until smooth. Place chopped nuts in shallow dish. Insert small candy cane into each marshmallow and dip end into chocolate. Dip into nuts and set on its side on waxed paper. Repeat. Store in covered container.

"My family looks forward to this traditional Christmas treat every year (so does Santa!)."

Shirley Blough   **Hillside Jr. High School, Simi Valley**

PRALINE POPCORN

Serves 10 to 12

10 cups popped corn
1½ cups whole pecans
½ cup slivered almonds
1⅓ cup sugar
1 cup butter

¼ cup praline liqueur
¼ cup light corn syrup
1 tablespoon praline liqueur
¼ teaspoon salt

Mix popcorn and nuts into a large bowl. Combine sugar, butter, the ¼ cup liqueur, and corn syrup in saucepan. Cook over medium heat, stirring often until temperature reaches 275 degrees on candy thermometer. Remove from heat and quickly stir in the 1 tablespoon liqueur and salt. Pour over corn/nut mixture until evenly coated. Immediately spread on baking sheet. Let stand 1 hour. They break into bite-size pieces.

"This makes a great holiday party snack."

Jackie DeWald-Mason   **Helix High School, La Mesa**

ALMOND ROCA

2 cups sugar
1 teaspoon salt
½ cup water
1 cup butter

1 cup almonds, chopped
4 plain Hershey bars
2 tablespoons almonds,
  chopped, for garnish

Mix first 5 ingredients in heavy saucepan. Cook over medium high heat until candy thermometer reads 305 degrees. Pour out onto a greased cookie sheet. After candy has set for 10 minutes, place Hershey bars on top and let soften, then spread. Sprinkle with 2 tablespoons almonds, cool and crack with an ice pick.

"Can be made ahead and frozen for later use. Makes an excellent Christmas gift for a candy lover."

Carolyn Hamill   **Pierce High School, Arbuckle**

ALMOND TOFFEE

Makes one cookie sheet full

1 cup sugar
1 small package almonds,
  slivered

2 cubes butter or margarine
3 tablespoons water

Combine ingredients in heavy skillet at low heat till butter and sugar melt. Then turn heat to highest setting and stir constantly until mixture turns a rich toffee color. Turn out onto cookie sheet and spread thin. Cool and break into pieces.

"Easy and delicious. We prefer it to peanut brittle because it's so quick."

Peggy Himenes   **Actis Jr. High School, Bakersfield**

ENGLISH TOFFEE

Makes 4 pounds

1 pound (2¼ cups) sugar
1 pound butter
4 tablespoons water

1½ pounds milk chocolate
3 cups almonds, chopped

Boil the sugar and butter together a few minutes before adding the water. Add the water, 1 tablespoon at a time, stirring only in the middle of the pan. Using a candy thermometer, cook to the hard crack stage (300 degrees). It should be golden brown and harden when a drop is put into water. Pour the toffee onto 2 unbuttered cookie sheets and spread to desired thickness; cool. Melt chocolate in a double boiler and then spread over the toffee. Sprinkle with the chopped nuts. Cool and let harden. When cold, break into small pieces.

"Wonderful to give as holiday goodies. People beg for it each Christmas!"

Beverly Fincher-Ranger   **Carpinteria High School, Carpinteria**

QUICK ALMOND BRITTLE

Makes 2 pounds

3 cups sugar
½ cup butter
dash of salt

½ cup almonds, coarsely
  chopped
1 package (6 oz.) chocolate chips
½ cup almonds, finely chopped

Place sugar, butter, and salt in an electric skillet. Set temperature control to 400 degrees. When sugar begins to melt, stir to blend. Cook and stir until sugar dissolves and color is light golden brown (about 5 minutes). Turn control to OFF. Stir in coarsely chopped almonds. Pour into buttered 15 x 10" pan or onto buttered foil. Melt chocolate chips over low heat. Spread over hardened candy. Sprinkle with finely chopped almonds. Break into pieces when cool.

"Super easy and delicious. Makes a nice Christmas gift."

Kay Linberger   **Tokay High School, Lodi**

CASHEW BRICKLE IN WHITE CHOCOLATE LACE

1 cup butter (do not substitute)
1⅓ cups sugar
1 tablespoon light corn syrup

3 tablespoons water
1 cup cashews, toasted
32 ounces white chocolate coating or almond bark

Melt butter in a large pan. Add sugar, corn syrup, and water. Cook to 290 degrees on candy thermometer, stirring occasionally. Remove from heat and stir in cashews. Spread hot mixture into well-greased 13 x 9" pan. Cool. Turn candy out on waxed paper. Melt white chocolate over double boiler. When chocolate is smooth, put into pastry bag with writing tip. Squeeze chocolate in threads over candy to make lace effect. Let cool. Break with mallet and serve.

"Unusually good flavor. My quiet uncle roamed around our Christmas gathering to find where he could get the recipe. He must have loved it!"

Stephanie Zupanovich   **Kerman High School, Kerman**

Cheesecakes
Cheesecakes
Cheesecakes

KILLER CHEESECAKE

Serves 16

1½ cups crumbs (i.e.,graham
  crackers, chocolate waters,
  etc.)
¼ cup sugar
6 tablespoons butter or
  margarine
1 teaspoon cinnamon
5 packages (8 oz. each) cream
  cheese
1 cup sugar

4 eggs
1 tablespoon flavoring (I use
  mixture of orange and vanilla)
12 ounces semisweet chocolate,
  chopped; or mini semisweet
  chips
1½ teaspoons flour
1 jar (8 oz.) apricot/pineapple
  preserves

"Favorite crumb crust": Mix and pat first 4 ingredients into the bottom of a 10"
springform pan. Pat crumbs up the side of the pan approximately 1 inch.
Filling: In a mixer bowl, beat softened cream cheese until smooth. Beat in sugar,
eggs, flavorings. In a separate bowl, toss chocolate pieces with flour. Fold chocolate pieces into cream cheese mixture; pour into crust. Bake at 325 degrees for
approximately 1¼ hours until knife inserted in center brings back none of the
cake (chocolate **will** coat knife most likely). Cool. Top with heated preserves.
Refrigerate several hours or overnight.

*"This is a winner! It gets rave reviews every time. Can omit chocolate and
experiment with different flavorings, toppings, etc. Basic cream cheese, sugar,
and egg ingredients stay the same."*

Ellen Black-Eacker   **Nogales High School, La Puente**

HEAVENLY NO-BAKE CHEESECAKE

Serves 12

1½ cups chocolate wafer crumbs
  (about ¾ of 8 oz. package)
4 tablespoons butter or
  margarine, melted
1 envelope unflavored gelatin
1 cup milk
4 Milky Way bars (2.15 oz. each),
  sliced

2 packages (8 oz. each) cream
  cheese, softened
2 tablespoons sugar
1 teaspoon vanilla
1 cup (½ pint) heavy or whipping
  cream

Combine chocolate crumbs and butter; press into bottom and 2 inches up the sides of an 8" springform pan; chill. Sprinkle gelatin over milk in a medium saucepan. Stir over low heat until gelatin is dissolved. Add Milky Way bars and continue to stir over low heat until mixture is smooth; cool slightly. Meanwhile, beat cream cheese and sugar until smooth. Beat in Milky Way mixture and vanilla. Add cream and beat at high speed 4 minutes. Pour mixture into prepared crust. Chill until firm, about 4 hours. If desired, garnish with additional whipped cream and sliced Milky Way bars.

"This cheesecake is also good when served with a fresh strawberry sauce: puree 2 cups strawberries with 1 tablespoon sugar in a blender."

M & M Mars Company   **Accomac, Virginia**

KAHLUA FANTASY CHOCOLATE CHEESECAKE

Serves 12 to 16

1⅓ cups chocolate wafers, crushed
1 tablespoon sugar
¼ cup butter, melted
¼ cup Kahlua
1½ cups semisweet chocolate chips
2 tablespoons butter
2 eggs

⅓ cup sugar
¼ teaspoon salt
1 cup sour cream
2 packages (8 oz. each) cream cheese
Chocolate Topping (optional):
1 cup chocolate chips
⅓ cup each Kahlua and light corn syrup

Crust: In a 9" springform pan, mix first three ingredients and press into bottom and sides with fork.

Filling: Cook Kahlua, chocolate chips, and butter in a saucepan till smooth. Set aside to cool. Beat eggs in a small bowl. Using mixer, beat in sugar and salt, then sour cream. Drop cream cheese in small pieces into mixture and beat till smooth. Gradually beat in chocolate mixture. Turn into pan over crust. Bake at 325 degrees for 40 minutes. Remove from oven; let stand at room temperature for 1 hour; refrigerate for several hours.

Topping: Heat ingredients in saucepan until chocolate melts. Cool. Spoon over cheesecake slices.

"I got this recipe from my friend Karen Bennett, who now teaches Home Economics at Norco High School. This is a wonderful recipe which I usually serve after low calorie meals in order to reduce any feelings of guilt."

Pam Amelotte   **Ocean View High School, Huntington Beach**

CHOCOLATE MOCHA CHEESECAKE

Serves 10 to 12

*1¼ cup chocolate wafer cookie
    crumbs*
¼ cup sugar
¼ cup butter, melted
*1 package (8 oz.) cream cheese,
    softened*

1 can (14 oz.) Eagle brand milk
⅔ cup chocolate syrup
2 tablespoons instant coffee
1 teaspoon hot water
1 cup whipping cream, whipped

Crust: Combine crumbs, sugar, and butter in food processor. Pat crumb mixture into a springform pan, bottom and sides.

Filling: Beat cheese with an electric mixer until fluffy. Add milk and syrup. In a small bowl, dissolve coffee in water and add to cheese mixture. Fold in whipped cream. Pour into pan. Freeze 6 hours or overnight. Garnish with extra chocolate crumbs or fresh raspberries. Return leftovers to the freezer.

"Always a hit and super easy!"

Gail McAuley   **Lincoln High School, Stockton**

CHOCOLATE CHEESECAKE

Serves 16

*1 package (8 oz.) chocolate
    wafers*
⅓ cup butter, melted
2 tablespoons sugar
½ teaspoon nutmeg
3 eggs
1 cup sugar
*3 packages (8 oz. each) cream
cheese, softened*

*12 oz. semisweet chocolate,
    melted*
1 teaspoon vanilla
⅛ teaspoon salt
1 cup sour cream
1 cup heavy cream (optional)
*2 tablespoons confectioners'
    sugar (optional)*

Crust: Finely crush wafers in blender or food processor; combine them with the butter, 2 tablespoons sugar, and nutmeg. Press evenly over sides and bottom of a 9" springform pan. Refrigerate.

Filling: Preheat oven to 350 degrees. In a large bowl, beat eggs and sugar at high speed until light. Beat in cream cheese until smooth. Add melted chocolate, vanilla, salt, and sour cream, beating until smooth. Turn into crumb crust and bake approximately 1 hour, or until cheesecake is just firm when pan is gently shaken. Cool in pan on wire rack, then refrigerate overnight. Remove sides of pan.

Garnish: If desired, beat cream with confectioners' sugar until stiff and spread on top of cheesecake.

"This extremely rich cheesecake must be served in small portions. It's always a hit at potlucks!"

Myrna Swearingen   **Corona High School, Corona**

MOCHA CHOCOLATE CHIP CHEESECAKE

Serves 8 to 12

2¼ cups graham cracker crumbs
2 cups (one 12 oz. package)
  little bits semisweet chocolate
⅔ cup butter, melted
½ cup milk
4 teaspoons freeze-dried coffee

1 envelope unflavored gelatin
2 packages (8 oz. each) cream
  cheese, softened
1 can (14 oz.) sweetened
  condensed milk
2 cups heavy cream, whipped

Crust: In bowl, combine graham cracker crumbs, 1 cup chocolate bits, and melted butter; mix well. Pat into 9" springform pan, covering bottom and 2½" up the sides; set aside.

Filling: In saucepan, combine milk and freeze dried coffee; sprinkle gelatin on top. Set aside for one minute. Then cook over low heat, stirring constantly until gelatin and coffee dissolve. Set aside. In bowl, beat cream cheese until creamy. Beat in sweetened condensed milk and gelatin mixture. Fold in remaining 1 cup chocolate bits and whipped cream; pour into prepared pan. Chill and serve.

"For all cheesecake lovers!"

Joanne Fial   **East Middle School, Downey**

CHOCOLATE CHIP CHEESECAKE

Serves 10 to 12

1 cup crushed creme filled
  cookies (about 12)
2 tablespoons butter, melted
3 packages (8 oz.) cream cheese,
  softened

½ cup brown sugar, packed
1 teaspoon vanilla
4 eggs
¾ cup chocolate chips

Crust: Combine cookie crumbs and butter; press onto bottom of 9" springform pan. Bake at 350 degrees for 10 minutes.

Filling: Combine cream cheese, sugar, and vanilla, mixing at medium speed until well blended. Add eggs, one at a time, mixing well after each addition. Stir in chocolate chips and pour over crust. Bake for 45 minutes more.

"Always a hit!"

Joy Aiello   **Liberty High School, Brentwood**

PERFECT CHEESECAKE

Serves 12 to 16

1¼ cup graham cracker crumbs
2 tablespoons sugar
3 tablespoons butter or
    margarine, melted
3 packages (8 oz. each) cream
    cheese or Neufchatel cheese

3 eggs
¾ cup sugar
1½ teaspoon vanilla
1 cup sour cream
2 tablespoons sugar
1 teaspoon vanilla

Crust: Mix crumbs, 2 tablespoons sugar, and melted butter together. Press mixture evenly in bottom of 9" springform pan.
Filling: Preheat oven to 375 degrees. Soften cheese and thoroughly blend until smooth the eggs, one at a time, sugar, and vanilla on low speed. Pour cheese mixture over crust. Bake at 375 degrees for 30 to 40 minutes or until center is firm, but "jiggly."
Topping: Combine sour cream, 2 tablespoons sugar, and 1 teaspoon vanilla; pour over cheesecake. Bake at 475 degrees for 5 minutes. Chill. Serve at room temperature.

"This is an all-time favorite of my entire family. Because Neufchatel cheese is lower in fat then cream cheese, you just might have seconds."

Barbara Adams   **Merced High School-North Campus, Merced**

MY FAVORITE CHEESECAKE

Serves 8

2 packages (8 oz. each) cream
    cheese, room temperature
½ cup sugar
2 eggs, room temperature

1 teaspoon vanilla
2 tablespoons sugar
1 cup sour cream
1 9" graham cracker crust

Cream together the cheese ½ cup sugar. Add eggs and vanilla to mixture and mix until smooth. Pour into prepared graham cracker crust and bake at 300 degrees for 20 minutes. Remove from oven and cool. Mix sugar and sour cream together and spread onto cheesecake. Bake for 5 more minutes, then refrigerate for 12 hours before serving.

"This recipe is everyone's favorite. I never reveal how easy it is!"

Linda Barnett   **Matilija Jr. High School, Ojai**

PRALINE CHEESECAKE

Serves 12 to 16

1 cup graham cracker crumbs
¼ cup pecans, finely ground
¼ cup brown sugar
¼ cup margarine, melted
3 packages (8 oz. each) cream
    cheese, softened

1¼ cup dark brown sugar
3 tablespoons flour
3 large eggs
2 teaspoons vanilla
⅓ cup pecans, finely chopped

Crust: Preheat oven to 350 degrees. Combine crumbs, ¼ cup sugar, and margarine, and press it into the bottom of a springform pan. Bake crust at 350 degrees for 10 minutes, or until firm.

Filling: Combine the cream cheese, 1¼ cup brown sugar, and flour until well blended. Add eggs, one at a time, mixing well after each. Blend in vanilla and nuts. Pour mixture over crumbs. Bake at 350 degrees for 50 to 60 minutes. Loosen cake from rim of pan and cool cake before removing from the pan sides. Chill, then garnish top with maple syrup and pecan halves.

"This is a recipe from Anna Rae Conan, who teaches computers at Sowers. This is one of the recipes that she prepared as a treat for the staff."

Susan Brown   **Sowers Middle School, Huntington Beach**

CINDY'S CHEESECAKE

Serves 8

1¼ cups graham cracker crumbs
¼ cup sugar
¼ cup margarine, melted
2 packages (8 oz. each) cream
  cheese, softened
1 cup sugar

3 eggs
1½ tablespoons lemon juice
1 carton (16 oz.) sour cream
½ cup sugar
1 teaspoon vanilla

Crust: Mix graham cracker crumbs, ¼ cup sugar and margarine together and press into bottom of 8 or 9" springform pan.

Filling: Cream the cheese and 1 cup sugar until smooth. Beat in one egg at a time, beating one minute between each egg. Add lemon juice and blend. Pour over crust. Bake at 325 to 350 degrees for 45 minutes.

Topping: Mix together the sour cream, ½ cup sugar, and vanilla. Pour topping on cheesecake and bake for an additional 15 minutes.

"This recipe was given to me by my sister-in-law a few years ago and has been a family favorite ever since."

Diana Lee   **Elsinore Jr. High School, Lake Elsinore**

CHEESECAKE PIE

Serves 8

1 cup Zwieback crumbs
¼ cup margarine, melted
2 tablespoons sugar
½ teaspoon cinnamon
  (optional)
2 packages (8 oz. each) cream
  cheese, softened
2 eggs

¾ cup sugar
2 teaspoons vanilla
½ teaspoon lemon peel, grated
1 cup sour cream, room
  temperature
2 tablespoons sugar
2 teaspoons vanilla

Crust: Combine the first four ingredients and press into the bottom and sides of a 9" pie pan. Chill.

Filling: Beat cream cheese slightly. Add eggs, ¾ cup sugar, 2 teaspoons vanilla, and lemon peel; beat until light and fluffy. Pour into crust. Bake at 350 degrees for 25 minutes or until firm. Cool cake in the oven with the door open for 1 hour.

Topping (prepare while pie bakes): Blend sour cream, 2 teaspoons sugar, and 2 teaspoons vanilla. Spread carefully over cooled cake. Refrigerate several hours.

"The Zwieback crust gives a light delicate taste I prefer to the graham cracker crust. The pie is very easy to make."

Jan Neufeld   **Fullerton High School, Fullerton**

CREAMIEST CHEESECAKE

Serves 6 to 8

16 graham crackers	*½ cup plus 3 tablespoons sugar*
5 tablespoons butter	*1 pint sour cream*
dash cinnamon	*2 eggs, slightly beaten*
1 package (8 oz.) cream cheese	*1 teaspoon vanilla*

Crust: Crush graham crackers until fine, stir in butter and cinnamon until well blended. Pat into pie pan.

Filling: Mix together cream cheese and ½ cup sugar. Add half the sour cream and mix until blended. Add eggs and vanilla. Pour into pie shell and bake at 350 degrees for 20 minutes. Allow to cool enough to spread on the topping.

Topping: Mix remaining half of sour cream with 3 tablespoons sugar and spread evenly on top. Bake for another 10 minutes. Best to chill overnight.

"So easy and so good. Everyone loves it!"

Sharon Hansen   **Rancho Buena Vista High School, Vista**

FISH BOAT CHEESECAKE

Serves 8

1 cup graham cracker crumbs	*2 eggs*
5 tablespoons butter or	*1 cup sour cream*
margarine, melted	*1 teaspoon vanilla*
12 oz. cream cheese	*2 tablespoons powdered sugar*
½ cup sugar	*fresh strawberries or other fruit*
1 tablespoon lemon juice	*for topping, sliced*

Crust: Mix graham crackers and melted butter. Press into 9" round pie plate.

Filling: Mix cream cheese, sugar, lemon juice, and eggs till smooth. Pour into crust. Mix sour cream, vanilla, powdered sugar together. Pour on top of cheese mixture. Bake at 325 degrees for 40 minutes. Cool and refrigerate.

Top with fresh sliced strawberries or fruit of your choice.

"This recipe was developed and used at our Fish Boat Restaurant in San Luis Obispo which we operated in the early 1980s!"

Mary E. Richmond   **San Luis Obispo High School, San Luis Obispo**

MACADAMIA NUT CHEESECAKE

Serves 8

1 cube butter, softened
¼ cup brown sugar
1 cup flour
½ cup macadamia nuts
1 package (8 oz.) cream cheese
½ cup sugar

1 teaspoon vanilla
1 cup whipping cream
⅓ cup macadamia nuts, finely
   chopped
2 tablespoons fudge syrup

Crumb Crust: Mix butter, brown sugar, flour, and ½ cup macadamia nuts together. Spread evenly into sheet pan. Bake at 350 degrees for 15 minutes until golden brown. While crumb mixture is still warm, mold into an 8" pie pan. Cool.
Filling: Beat cream cheese, sugar, and vanilla together until smooth. Whip cream until smooth. Fold cream cheese into the whipping cream. Spread filling into cooled pie crust. Sprinkle chopped macadamia nuts on top and drizzle fudge over top. Chill 1 hour.

"Eat slowly and enjoy. Chopped macadamias can be mixed into the filling too, if desired."

Penny Putnam   **Divisadero Middle School, Visalia**

QUICK AND EASY CHEESECAKE

Serves 8

1 package (8 oz.) cream cheese,
   softened
1 tablespoon lemon juice
½ teaspoon vanilla
2 eggs

½ cup sugar
prepared graham cracker crust
1 cup sour cream
2 tablespoons sugar
½ teaspoon vanilla

Combine cream cheese, lemon juice, and vanilla. Beat until creamy. Add the eggs, one at a time, with ½ cup sugar. Continue beating until smooth. Place filling in prepared crust. Bake at 325 degrees about 25 to 30 minutes until firm.
Topping: Mix sour cream, 2 tablespoons sugar, and vanilla. Smooth over baked filling. Continue to bake for 10 more minutes. Refrigerate for 3 to 4 hours.

Dianne Sheats   **Gridley High School, Gridley**

RITZ CRACKER CHEESECAKE

Serves 12

3 egg whites
28 Ritz crackers, crushed
¾ cup nuts, chopped
1 cup sugar
½ teaspoon baking powder
½ teaspoon vanilla

1 envelope Dream Whip
½ cup cold milk
½ teaspoon vanilla
8 oz. cream cheese, softened
1 cup crushed pineapple, drained

Crust: Whip the egg whites to medium stiffness. Add to crushed Ritz crackers. Add the nuts, sugar, baking powder, and vanilla until thoroughly combined. Spread into a square 8" greased pan. Bake at 350 degrees for ½ hour; cool.

Topping: Blend the Dream Whip, milk, and vanilla in a deep narrow bowl and beat at high speed for 4 minutes until very thick. In another bowl, whip the cream cheese until smooth; add the drained pineapple and then the Dream Whip. Spread on top of cooled cake layer and chill in refrigerator.

"Compliments of Ritz crackers."

Jill Sweet Anderson   **Santa Paula Union High School, Santa Paula**

QUICK LEMON CHEESECAKE

Serves 8

2 envelopes unflavored gelatin	*1 package (8 oz.) cream cheese*
3 tablespoons lemon juice	*½ cup whipping cream*
grated rind of 1 lemon	*1 tablespoon vanilla*
½ cup hot water	*10 to 12 ice cubes*
⅔ cup sugar	*1 graham cracker prepared crust*
2 egg yolks	*½ cup graham cracker crumbs*

Place gelatin, lemon juice, rind, and hot water in blender and whir for 45 seconds. Add sugar, egg yolks, and cream cheese, and blend another 10 seconds. Add cream and vanilla and whir again 10 seconds. Add ice cubes, one at a time, and blend till dissolved. Will set up quickly, so pour at once into crust and sprinkle with cracker crumbs. Ready to serve immediately, but keeps nicely for several days. Refrigerate.

"Light, airy, and so quick. The cook loves to do it, and everyone loves to eat it!"

Charlotte Heitzmann   **Mariposa City High School, Mariposa**

RASPBERRY CHEESECAKE

Serves 10 to 12

1⅔ cups graham cracker crumbs	*1 teaspoon vanilla*
¼ cup sugar	*2 eggs*
¼ cup butter, melted	*1 package frozen raspberries,*
2 packages (8 oz. each) cream	*thawed*
cheese, softened	*2 tablespoons cornstarch*
½ cup sugar	

Crust: Combine first 3 ingredients and press into 7 x 12" pan. Bake at 375 degrees for 8 minutes.

Filling: Beat together softened cream cheese, sugar, vanilla, and eggs, one at a time. Pour over cooled crust and bake at reduced 350 degrees heat for 20 minutes. Cool.

Topping: Mash up raspberries and cook with cornstarch until they begin to thicken. Cool and spread on top of cheesecake.

Cheryl Pullan   **Terrace Hills Jr. High School, Grand Terrace**

CHERRY CHEESECAKE

Serves 12 to 15

2¼ cups graham cracker crumbs
⅔ cup margarine, melted
2 cups sugar, divided
2 packages (8 oz. each) cream
  cheese, softened

4 eggs
2 cans (15 oz. each) cherry pie
  filling

Crust: Mix together the graham cracker crumbs, margarine, and 1 cup sugar. Pour into a 9 x 12" baking dish. Use a fork to pat the crust firm and flat.
Filling: Beat the cream cheese with a mixer; add 1 cup sugar and beat until well blended and smooth. Add eggs, one at a time, continuing to beat. The filling should be a creamy color and completely smooth. Bake at 325 degrees for 25 minutes. Allow to cool. Top with pie filling.

"My mom's favorite dessert. It's great for family reunions and potluck dinners. Can be cut in half and baked in a 9" square pan."

Tena Raglin   **Dos Palos High School, Dos Palos**

PINEAPPLE CHEESECAKE

Serves 12

18 graham crackers
¼ pound butter, melted
1 package (8 oz.) cream cheese
1 package (3 oz.) cream cheese
½ cup sugar
2 eggs, well beaten

2 teaspoons vanilla
1 can (20 oz.) pineapple, crushed
  and well drained
dash cinnamon
1 pint sour cream
2 tablespoons sugar

Crust: Roll crackers into fine crumbs and mix well with butter. Press into a 10" springform pan; set aside.
Filling: Cream the cream cheese and sugar. Add eggs and 1 teaspoon vanilla and beat. Stir in pineapple and cinnamon. Pour into cracker lined pan and bake at 375 degrees about 25 minutes, until center is set. Remove from oven and cool for 5 minutes.
Topping: Mix sour cream, sugar, and 1 teaspoon vanilla. Spoon over top of baked filling. Bake at 500 degrees for 2 minutes. Let cool. Chill in refrigerator before serving.

Amber Bradley   **El Capitan High School, Lakeside**

BLUEBERRY DESSERT

Serves 12 to 13

20 graham crackers
½ cup sugar
1 cube margarine, softened
1 package (8 oz.) cream cheese
2 eggs

1 teaspoon vanilla
1 cup sugar
1 can blueberry pie filling
1 tablespoon lemon juice

Crust: Roll the crackers into fine crumbs. Mix with sugar and margarine. Pack evenly into a 9 x 13" pan.

Filling: Beat cream cheese; add eggs, vanilla, and sugar and beat until fluffy. Spread on cracker mixture and bake at 375 degrees for 20 minutes. Cool.

Topping: Combine blueberries with lemon juice. Heat to simmering; then cool. Spread over cheese mixture. Cool and chill well.

Donna Malbon   **Rowland High School, Rowland Heights**

PEACH CARROT CHEESECAKE

Serves 12

1 package carrot cake mix
½ cup oil
2 cans (16 oz. each) peach halves, drained and reserve liquid
1 envelope unflavored gelatin
2 packages (8 oz. each) cream cheese

1 can sweetened condensed milk
2 tablespoons lemon juice
4 ounces frozen non-dairy whipped topping, thawed
1 teaspoon cornstarch
mint leaves

Crust: Preheat oven to 350 degrees. Grease a 10" springform pan. Combine dry cake mix and oil in bowl; mix well. Turn into pan and spread evenly. Bake at 350 degrees for 20 minutes. Cool; then refrigerate.

Filling: Drain peaches, reserving 1 cup juice. Combine ½ cup of juice with gelatin in saucepan. Cook over low heat, stirring constantly until gelatin dissolves. Reserve 3 peach halves for garnish. Puree remaining peaches in blender until smooth. Combine peaches and gelatin mixture; set aside. Beat cream cheese until smooth in large bowl. Add condensed milk and lemon juice; mix well. Stir in peach gelatin mixture. Fold in whipped topping. Turn into crust-lined pan and spread evenly.

To decorate, slice reserved peaches and arrange in 2-piece clusters on top of cheesecake For glaze, blend remaining ½ cup peach juice and cornstarch in saucepan. Cook and stir until mixture boils and thickens; cool. Spoon cooled glaze evenly over cheesecake. Add mint leaves to peach clusters. Refrigerate at least 3 hours before serving.

"This unusual blend of ingredients produces a family favorite that is very beautiful, festive, and delicious."

Claudia J. Armstead   **Jefferson Middle School, Long Beach**

RICH 'N WONDERFUL PUMPKIN CHEESECAKE

Makes 2 9" pies

2 pounds cream cheese
1½ cups sugar
3 eggs
1 cup whipping cream
1 pound canned pumpkin

2 teaspoons vanilla
1 tablespoon pumpkin pie spice
2 graham cracker prepared crusts
sour cream (optional)

Blend cream cheese with sugar until smooth. Add eggs, one at a time, beating until blended. Add whipping cream, canned pumpkin, vanilla, and spice, blending thoroughly. Pour into two crusts. Bake at 325 degrees approximately 1½ hours or until set. Cool thoroughly before removing from pan. Chill and serve with sour cream, if desired.

"Forget counting calories on this one. Just eat and enjoy."

Gloria King   **Schurr High School, Montebello**

PETITE CHERRY CHEESECAKES

Yields 1 dozen individual cakes

1 package (8 oz.) cream cheese,
   softened
¼ cup plus 2 tablespoons sugar
1 egg

1½ teaspoon lemon juice
½ teaspoon vanilla
12 vanilla wafers
½ can cherry pie filling

Beat together cream cheese, sugar, egg, lemon juice, and vanilla until light and fluffy. Line small muffin pans with 12 paper cups; place a vanilla wafer in bottom of each. Fill cups ⅔ full with cheese mixture. Bake at 375 degrees for 15 minutes or just until set. Top each with about 1 tablespoon cherry pie filling; chill.

"Recipe may be doubled. This are yummy little cheesecakes."

Barbara Hansen   **Montclair High School, Montclair**

MINI CHEESECAKE DELIGHTS

Makes 20

2 packages (8 oz. each) cream
   cheese, softened
1 tablespoon lemon juice
1 teaspoon vanilla

¾ cup sugar
2 eggs
20 vanilla wafers
1 can (21 oz.) cherry pie filling

Preheat oven to 350 degrees. Cream together until smooth, the softened cream cheese, lemon juice, vanilla, sugar, and eggs. Place 1 cupcake paper liner into each hole in a muffin tin. Place 1 vanilla wafer in the bottom of each paper liner. Fill paper liner ¾ full of batter. Bake for 10 to 15 minutes, or until a sharp blade knife comes out clean. Let cool. Top with cherry pie filling (about 3 cherries with juice, or 1 tablespoon on each).

"This is great for Valentine's Day! My students rated this a 10."

Nancy O'Brien   **Buena High School, Ventura**

TERESA'S CHEESECAKE CUPCAKES

Makes 24 cupcakes

*3 packages (8 oz. each) cream
  cheese
5 eggs
½ cup butter or margarine
1½ teaspoons vanilla*

*1 cup sugar
fresh or frozen berries
cornstarch or tapioca for
  thickener
1 pint sour cream*

Mix well the first 5 ingredients. Pour into 24 lined cupcake tins. Bake at 300 degrees for 40 minutes. Remove from oven and let cool 5 minutes. A dent will form...fill dent with fresh berries thickened with cornstarch or tapioca. Top with sour cream (may be sweetened to taste). Return to oven and bake for another 5 minutes.

Kathleen Daudistel   **Hanford High School, Hanford**

Cookies
Cookies
Cookies

Luscious Lemon Layer Torte, Page 95
Banana and Brandy Parfait, Page 141
Cherries Jubilee on Ice Cream, Page 96

Trifle of Macaroons and Ladyfingers, Page 97

Frosted Cafe au Lait, Page 92   **Terrific Strawberry Soda, Page 90**

California Chocolate Bars, Page 83

PETTICOAT TAILS

Makes 3 dozen

2 cups margarine, softened
1 cup powdered sugar
1 teaspoon vanilla

2½ cups flour
¼ teaspoon salt
colored sugar to sprinkle

Mix all ingredients together. Then use hands to make 2 rolls (use as little flour as possible). Wrap and put into refrigerator overnight. Slice ¼" thick and bake on cookie sheets at 400 degrees for 8 to 10 minutes. Watch carefully as they have a tendency to burn. Sprinkle with colored sugar for a different look. These cookies are hard to handle. I freeze one roll and bake it later. It is easier this way.

"These delicious cookies literally melt in your mouth."

Cathy Miller   **Montclair High School, Montclair**

COFFEE CAKE COOKIES

Makes 3 to 3½ dozen

4 cups flour
1 teaspoon salt
1¼ cups sugar
2 cups margarine
1 package yeast

¼ cup warm water
1 cup scalded milk, cooled
2 eggs, beaten
1 tablespoon cinnamon
buttercream frosting

Combine flour, salt, and ¼ cup sugar. Cut in margarine. Dissolve yeast in water and combine with milk and eggs. Add this to flour mixture and mix into a dough ball. Cover with foil and refrigerate overnight. Divide dough in half and roll each half to a 12 x 18 rectangle. Sprinkle mixture of 1 cup sugar and 1 tablespoon cinnamon on rolled out dough. Roll up long side and pinch edges. Cut into 1" slices. Place cut side down on cookie sheet. Bake at 400 degrees for 12 minutes. Cool for 5 minutes and frost with buttercream frosting.

"These are great for brunch or as a snack. Everyone that samples them, loves them."

Vicki A. Pearl   **Giano Jr. High School, La Puente**

SCOOBY SNACKS

Makes 4 to 5 dozen cookies

1 cup butter or margarine
2 cups all purpose flour
⅓ cup whipping cream
sugar to sprinkle

Cream Filling:
¼ cup soft butter or margarine
¾ cup confectioners' sugar
1 teaspoon vanilla
1 or 2 drops food coloring

Cream butter or margarine with flour. After thoroughly mixed, add cream slowly mixing as you add. Once it is mixed together, cover and chill for 1 hour. Roll dough on lightly floured surface ⅛" thick. Cut out 2" round cookies, using a cookie cutter. Place on ungreased cookie sheet. Sprinkle with sugar. Prick in 4 rows with fork. Bake at 375 degrees for 7 to 9 minutes.

Cream filling: Blend butter or margarine and sugar. Add vanilla. Tint with the food coloring, if desired. After the cookies cool, spread the filling on one and then top with another cookie for a "cookie sandwich."

"My son, Willy, named these cookies when he was 3 years old. He could pop them in his mouth as fast as I could make them."

Melody Mayfield   **Las Plumas High School, Oroville**

OATMEAL/PEANUT BUTTER COOKIES

Makes 2 to 3 dozen

¼ cup margarine
½ cup peanut butter
⅓ cup sugar
⅓ cup brown sugar
2 eggs
1 teaspoon vanilla

1¼ cups whole wheat flour
½ teaspoon salt
1 teaspoon baking soda
3 cups quick cooking oats
½ cup raisins
½ cup chocolate chips

Cream margarine, peanut butter, sugars, eggs, and vanilla. Add wheat flour, salt, and baking soda. Mix well. Gradually add quick cooking oats, raisins, and chocolate chips. These can be rolled and refrigerated and then sliced and baked as needed, or dropped by tablespoonfuls onto cookie sheet. (The raw dough freezes well.) Bake at 350 degrees for 10 to 12 minutes.

"This recipe was developed by the students from a basic oatmeal recipe."

Barsha Elzey   **Terra Linda High School, San Rafael**

SOFT AND CHEWY MOLASSES COOKIES

Makes 30 cookies

¼ cup vegetable oil
¼ cup molasses
1¼ cups sugar
2 eggs
2¾ cups flour

1½ teaspoons baking soda
1 teaspoon cinnamon
1 teaspoon ginger
¼ teaspoon ground cloves
sugar for coating

In a large bowl, stir together oil, molasses, and 1 cup sugar. Add eggs and beat until smooth. In another bowl, stir together flour, baking soda, and spices, and gradually add to molasses mixture, beating until well combined. Cover tightly and refrigerate for at least one hour. Place remaining ¼ cup sugar in a small bowl. Roll dough into 1½" balls, then roll in sugar to coat. Place 3 inches apart on greased cookie sheet. Bake at 350 degrees for 10 to 12 minutes or until lightly browned. Transfer to racks and let cool.

Angela Croce   **Mira Mesa High School, San Diego**

LEMON SNAPS

Makes 5 dozen

¾ cup butter or margarine	*2 cups flour, sifted*
1¼ cups sugar	*1 teaspoon baking powder*
1 egg	*½ teaspoon salt*
½ teaspoon vanilla	*¼ teaspoon baking soda*
½ teaspoon lemon extract	*2 tablespoons lemon rind, grated*
¼ cup milk	

Cream together butter and ¾ cup sugar. Beat in egg, vanilla, lemon extract, and milk. Sift in flour baking powder, salt, baking soda (a little at a time), blending well. Chill one hour or until firm. Form into marble-sized balls. Roll in mixture of remaining ½ cup sugar and lemon rind to coat well. Bake at 350 degrees for 8 to 10 minutes on ungreased cookie sheet 2 inches apart until edges are slightly brown.

Linda Robinson   **Sinaloa Jr. High School, Simi Valley**

GRANDMA'S SCOTCH SHORTBREAD

Makes 2 dozen

½ cup butter or Imperial	*1 egg yolk*
* margarine*	*1⅛ cups flour*
⅓ cup sugar	

Cream butter and sugar. Beat in egg yolk. Stir in flour. Shape into a 1½" roll on plastic wrap or wax paper. Wrap well and refrigerate at least 2 hours. Preheat oven to 325 degrees. Slice dough into ¼" slices. Place 1" apart on ungreased baking sheet and bake for 15 to 20 minutes, or until edges are lightly browned.

"An old family recipe from my mother-in-law. These cookies keep and mail well."

Cheryl Dozier   **Nova High School, Redding**

COCONUT THUMBPRINT COOKIES

Makes about 54 cookies

1 cup butter or margarine
¼ teaspoon salt
1 cup confectioners' sugar, sifted
1 teaspoon almond extract
  (optional)
1¾ cups flour, unsifted

1 cup coconut, flaked
¾ cup blanched almonds,
  ground or finely chopped
  (optional)
jelly, jam, marmalade, or
preserves

Cream butter with salt. Gradually beat in sugar. Blend in almond extract. Add flour, a small amount at a time, mixing well after each addition. Stir in coconut and almonds. Chill dough; then roll a small amount at a time into small balls. Place on ungreased baking sheets. Bake at 325 degrees for 8 minutes. Remove from oven and make a depression in center of each with thumb or measuring spoon. Return to oven and bake 12 to 15 minutes longer, or until lightly browned. Cool on sheets; then fill each cookie with 1 teaspoon jelly. Sprinkle with more coconut, if desired. Store in loosely covered jar.

"These cookies are very easy to make, yet look like they are difficult. An elegant touch to any dessert."

Karen Ross   **Demille Middle School, Long Beach**

FAIRY DROPS

Makes 5 dozen

1 cup butter
1 cup powdered sugar
1 cup oil
2 eggs
1 teaspoon vanilla

4½ cups flour plus 2 tablespoons
1 teaspoon soda
1 teaspoon salt
1 teaspoon cream of tartar
1 cup sugar

Cream butter and powdered sugar together until fluffy. Blend in oil; beat until fluffy. Add eggs and beat well. Add vanilla, flour, soda, salt, cream of tartar; blend until well mixed. Chill dough. Roll dough in balls the size of walnuts. Roll balls in sugar, place on ungreased cookie sheet, and bake at 350 degrees for 15 minutes. Remove from cookie sheet and cool on rack.

"Cookies melt in your mouth. I roll cookie dough in a combination of cinnamon, not just sugar ... it adds to the taste."

Nadean Rona   **Columbus High School, Downey**

FUDGE MELTAWAYS

Makes about 25 small cookies

3/4 cup butter
2 1/2 squares (2 1/2 oz.)
   unsweetened chocolate
1/4 cup sugar
2 teaspoons vanilla, divided
1 egg, beaten

2 cups graham crackers
1 cup coconut
1/2 cup nuts, chopped
1 tablespoon milk
2 cups powdered sugar, sifted

Melt 1/2 cup butter and 1 square chocolate in saucepan. Add sugar, vanilla, egg, crumbs, coconut, and nuts into the butter mixture. Mix well and press into an ungreased square 8" pan. Refrigerate. Mix 1/4 cup butter, milk, powdered sugar, and 1 teaspoon vanilla. Spread over crumb mixture. Chill. Melt 1 1/2 squares chocolate and spread a thin layer over the chilled filling evenly. Chill again. Then cut into tiny squares before completely firm.

"A Christmas favorite!"

Beverly Fincher-Ranger   **Carpinteria High School, Carpinteria**

BESS' SUGAR COOKIES

Makes 4 dozen

1 cup powdered sugar
1 cup granulated sugar
2 cubes margarine
1 cup oil
2 eggs

4 1/2 cups flour
1 teaspoon soda
1 teaspoon cream of tartar
1 teaspoon flavoring (either
   lemon or vanilla)

Mix all ingredients together and let stand a few minutes. Shape into balls. Flatten with water glass dipped in sugar. Bake at 350 degrees about 12 minutes till barely light brown around the edges.

"This family recipe makes a delicious light cookie."

Karen McCord   **Lindsay High School, Lindsay**

LEMON SUGAR COOKIES

Makes 30

2 cups flour
1 teaspoon baking powder
pinch salt
pinch nutmeg, grated
1/2 cup vegetable oil

1/2 cup sugar
1 egg
rind of 1 small lemon, grated
sugar

Nan Paul   **Grant Middle School, Escondido**

Sift together the flour, baking powder, salt, and nutmeg. Combine the oil and sugar in a bowl, then beat in the egg and lemon rind. Add the dry ingredients into the oil mixture and mix well. Shape into balls about ¾" in diameter. Dip the tops of the balls into sugar and place sugar side up on greased cookie sheets, about 2" apart. Press the tops of the cookies with the tines of a fork to make a criss-cross pattern. Bake in a preheated 375 degree oven for 10 to 12 minutes.

EASY PEANUT BUTTER COOKIES

Makes 2 to 3 dozen

1 cup chunky peanut butter
1 cup granulated sugar

1 egg, beaten
½ teaspoon vanilla

Mix peanut butter and sugar together. Stir in beaten egg and vanilla. Shape into 1" balls. Place on ungreased cookie sheet. Press with dinner fork to flatten slightly. Bake at 350 degrees for 12 to 15 minutes. Cool on wire rack. Shorter baking time will yield softer cookies.

"I didn't forget any ingredients! These cookies require NO flour! They are quick and easy to prepare for young and old alike."

Donna Geer   **Chino High School, Chino**

PEPPERMINT PUFFS

Makes about 3 to 4 dozen

⅔ cup butter-flavored Crisco
¼ cup sugar
¼ cup brown sugar, firmly
*   packed*
1 egg

1½ cups flour, unsifted
½ teaspoon baking powder
½ teaspoon salt
½ cup peppermint candy canes,
*   crushed*

Preheat oven to 350 degrees. Lightly grease baking sheets with butter-flavored Crisco. Cream butter-flavored Crisco and sugars in a large bowl at medium speed of electric mixer. Beat in egg. Combine flour, baking powder, and salt. Blend into creamed mixture and stir in crushed candy. Shape dough into small balls (about 1"). Bake for 11 to 12 minutes and remove to cooling racks.

"These dress up a cookie plate. They could work well with any flavor of hard candy ... we also like cherry."

Lucille Bell   **Palmdale High School, Palmdale**

IRRESISTIBLE GRANOLA COOKIES

Makes about 4 dozen

1 cup butter or margarine
1 cup brown sugar
1 cup sugar
2 eggs
1 teaspoon vanilla
2 cups unbleached flour
2 teaspoons baking powder
1 teaspoon salt (optional)

1 teaspoon baking soda
1 cup chocolate chips
1½ cups raisins (optional)
1½ cups walnuts
1 cup old fashioned rolled oats
2 cups Nectar-Sweet Crunchy Oat
  Bran Granola

Cream together butter and sugars. Beat the eggs and vanilla into the mixture. Sift together the flour, baking powder, salt, and baking soda. Add the dry ingredients to mixture; mix well. Stir in chocolate chips, raisins, nuts, oats, and granola. When well mixed, shape into golf ball size and bake on ungreased cookie sheet at 350 degrees for 8 to 10 minutes or until barely golden. Best when slightly undercooked and warm from the oven.

"Dough keeps well when refrigerated ... bake as needed."

Marilyn Pereira   **Hanford High School, Hanford**

PEANUT COOKIES

Makes 6 dozen

2 cups brown sugar
1 cup shortening
2 eggs
1 teaspoon vanilla
2½ cups oatmeal

1½ cups flour, sifted
1 teaspoon baking soda
½ teaspoon baking powder
1 cup coconut, shredded
1 cup salted spanish peanuts

Cream together brown sugar, shortening, eggs, and vanilla. Stir in oatmeal, flour, baking soda, baking powder; add coconut and peanuts last. Roll into 1" balls and place on cookie sheet. Cookies will flatten as they bake.

"These scrumptious cookies are a family favorite."

Myra Skidmore   **Downey High School, Downey**

MOCHA NUT BUTTERBALLS

Makes about 4 dozen

2 cups margarine, softened
½ cup sugar
2½ tablespoons Tia Maria
½ cup unsweetened cocoa

3½ cups flour
2 cups ground pecans
powdered sugar (optional)

Cream margarine and sugar with a wooden spoon. Add Tia Maria, cocoa, and flour. Mix well. Then stir in ground pecans. Shape into ¾" balls and place on a greased baking sheet 1" apart. Bake at 325 degrees for 15 minutes. Remove and cool on a rack. When cooled, roll in powdered sugar if desired.

Becky Tice   **Dana Hills High School, Dana Point**

PHENOMENAL PEANUT BUTTER CUPS

Makes 36

1 roll Pillsbury Slice 'n Bake
  peanut butter cookies

1 package Reese's miniature
  peanut butter cups

Cut cookie dough into 9 equal slices, then quarter each slice. Place dough into miniature muffin tins. Bake at 375 degrees for 8 minutes. As soon as cookies are removed from the oven, press an unwrapped peanut butter cup in the center of each. Refrigerate for 5 to 10 minutes.

"So easy and so good."

Glenell Fuller   **Glendora High School, Glendora**

SWEDISH ALMOND RUSKS

Makes about 120 rusks

5 cups flour
1 teaspoon baking soda
1 teaspoon salt
1 cup shortening
1¾ cups sugar

2 large eggs
1 tablespoon almond extract
1 cup sour cream
1 cup blanched almonds, minced

Sift flour with soda and salt. In large bowl, beat shortening until creamy; add sugar, about ⅓ at a time, beating well after each addition. When well blended, add eggs one at a time, beating well after each addition. Stir in extract. Mix in dry ingredients, about ⅓ at a time, alternating with sour cream (mixture will be stiff). Mix in almonds.

Turn out dough onto lightly floured board and knead lightly to make sure dough is well blended. Divide dough into 6 equal parts and shape each part into a cylinder about 15" long and 1" diameter. Place 3 rolls each on two ungreased baking sheets, leaving space between each roll. Bake at 350 degrees about 30 minutes, until lightly browned. Remove from oven and cut into ½" thick diagonal slices. Put slices back on cookie sheet 1" apart. Bake 20 minutes longer, until each slice is golden. Cool on wire racks.

"The rusks are a family Christmas favorite ... excellent with coffee or milk. Flavor develops with keeping. Recipe may be divided in half."

Barbara Adams   **Merced High School, Merced**

ITALIAN ANISE SLICES

Makes 3 to 4 dozen

3 cups flour, sifted
1 teaspoon salt
1 tablespoon baking powder
½ cup butter
1 cup sugar

1 teaspoon anise flavoring
3 eggs
1 cup walnuts, ground, or
  blanched almonds

Preheat oven to 350 degrees. Sift together dry ingredients. Cream together butter, sugar, and anise flavoring. Beat in eggs, one at a time. Add creamed mixture to flour mixture and blend. Stir in nuts. On a cookie sheet form 2 rectangles, approximately 10" long, 4" wide, and 1½" thick. Bake at 350 degrees until firm to touch, about 30 to 35 minutes. Turn off oven. Remove from oven and cool slightly. While warm, cut into slices about ½" thick and separate. Return to oven to dry out, about 10 to 20 minutes. Cool and store in a tin.

"My Slavonian grandmother, who emigrated to the U.S. when she was 19, kept these cookies in a special tin and served them with coffee to her guests. They are a great light dessert."

Maria Fregulia   **Lassen Union High School, Susanville**

LACY FUNNEL CAKES

Serves 6

vegetable oil for deep frying
2 large eggs
3 teaspoons vegetable oil
2 tablespoons sugar
1 teaspoon baking powder

1 teaspoon salt
⅔ cup milk
1½ cups flour
powdered sugar for dusting top

Pour oil into a heavy skillet to a depth of 2" and heat over medium heat. In a medium bowl, beat together all ingredients **except** the flour and powdered sugar. Gradually beat in the flour until the mixture is smooth. If the batter is too thick to pour, thin it by adding a tablespoon of milk at a time. Pour ¼ cup of batter into a funnel, keeping your finger over the opening of the funnel. Hold the funnel over the hot oil, remove your finger and swirl the batter starting in the center and working outward to make a 6" spiral. Then release the rest of the batter across the spiral to form a lacy pattern. Fry 1 to 2 minutes on each side until they are golden brown. Drain on paper towels and sprinkle with powdered sugar.

"We do this recipe in class all the time ... kids love it. It's great for a party and let the guests do their own."

Val Herford   **Sage Intermediate School, Palmdale**

PUMPKIN COOKIES

Makes about 5 dozen

1 cup shortening
2 cups sugar
2 cups canned pumpkin
1 teaspoon salt
2 teaspoons soda
2 teaspoons baking powder
2 teaspoons cinnamon
2 teaspoons vanilla

1 cup golden raisins
1 cup walnuts, chopped
4 cups flour
Glaze:
½ pound confectioners' sugar
2 to 3 tablespoons milk
½ teaspoon vanilla

Mix all cookie ingredients in order given. Drop by teaspoonfuls onto ungreased cookie sheet. Bake at 350 degrees for 15 to 20 minutes. Mix all glaze ingredients until a smooth consistency. Glaze cookies while still warm by dipping cookies into glaze.

"My mother gave me this recipe years ago. It continues to be a favorite, especially when served during Thanksgiving and Christmas."

Gerry Henderson   **Temple City High School, Temple City**

PERSIMMON COOKIES

Makes about 4 to 5 dozen

2¼ cups flour
1 teaspoon baking powder
1 teaspoon cinnamon
½ teaspoon cloves
½ teaspoon nutmeg
½ teaspoon salt
½ cup butter
⅓ cup brown sugar

1 cup sugar
1 egg
1 teaspoon soda
1 cup persimmon pulp
1 teaspoon vanilla
1 cup nuts, chopped
1 cup raisins

Sift together dry ingredients. Cream butter and sugars; add egg. Combine soda and pulp and mix in with creamed butter mixture. Add vanilla, nuts, and raisins. Add flour mixture and stir. Drop by teaspoonfuls on lightly greased cookie sheet. Bake at 375 degrees for 10 to 12 minutes.

Sally Oxford   **Monache High School, Porterville**

PEANUT CRISPIES

Makes 5 dozen

1 cup margarine, softened
⅔ cup creamy peanut butter
1⅓ cups sugar
⅔ cup brown sugar
2 eggs
1 teaspoon vanilla

2 cups flour
1 teaspoon baking soda
½ teaspoon salt
4 cups rice crispy cereal
2 cups chocolate chips

Preheat oven to 350 degrees. Cream margarine, peanut butter, and sugars with a wooden spoon. Stir in the eggs and vanilla. Mix until well blended. In a small bowl, combine flour, baking soda, and salt. Add to creamed mixture. Mix well. Stir in rice crispies and chocolate chips. Drop by rounded teaspoonfuls onto ungreased baking sheet. Bake for 10 to 12 minutes.

"A favorite of my foods classes."

Julie Shelburne   **Tulare Union High School, Tulare**

PEANUT BUTTER BRAN COOKIES

Makes 2 dozen cookies

½ cup butter or shortening	1¼ cups flour
½ cup peanut butter	¾ teaspoon soda
1 cup brown sugar	¼ teaspoon salt
2 eggs	1 cup unsalted peanuts, chopped
1 teaspoon vanilla	½ cup unprocessed bran

Thoroughly cream butter, peanut butter, sugar, eggs, and vanilla. Sift together dry ingredients; blend into creamed mixture. Blend in chopped peanuts and unprocessed bran. Drop onto ungreased cookie sheet, press down with glass dipped in unprocessed bran or sugar. Place 2 inches apart. Bake at 375 degrees for 10 to 12 minutes.

"Good protein and fiber content."

Catherine Diaz   **Exeter Union High School, Exeter**

WORLD'S BEST PEANUT BUTTER COOKIES

Makes 5 dozen

1 cup butter	2 cups flour, sifted
1 cup peanut butter	1 teaspoon soda
1 cup granulated sugar	1 package (6 oz.) semisweet
1 cup brown sugar, packed	chocolate chips
2 eggs	½ cup roasted peanuts, chopped

Cream butter and peanut butter. Gradually add sugars until they are blended. Add eggs, one at a time. Beat until smooth. Measure sifted flour and sift again with the baking soda. Add to the creamed mixture. Stir in chocolate chips and peanuts. Drop by teaspoonfuls onto a greased baking sheet and flatten slightly with back of spoon. Bake at 350 degrees for 10 to 12 minutes.

"The secret to this recipe is thoroughly blending the butter and peanut butter (I use natural).

Myrna Swearingen   **Corona High School, Corona**

HEARTY OAT/CHOCOLATE COOKIES

Makes 9 dozen cookies

1¾ cups Puritan oil	2 teaspoons baking powder
1 pound brown sugar	2 teaspoons baking soda
8 egg whites	12 ounces milk chocolate chips
2 teaspoons vanilla	1½ cups walnuts or pecans,
4 cups unbleached flour	chopped
1 pound oat bran (1 lb. box	
Quakers Oat Bran)	

Cream together oil and brown sugar. Add egg whites and vanilla. Mix together flour, oat bran, baking powder, and baking soda. Combine the two mixtures together. Stir in chocolate chips and nuts. Bake on ungreased cookie sheet, 2 inches apart at 375 degrees for 6 minutes.

"The family enjoys getting their oat bran in this yummy form. These are favorites for snacks and/or desserts."

Judie Huffman   **Mariposa County High School, Mariposa**

CHEWY OATMEAL COOKIES

Makes 3 to 4 dozen

1 cup flour
3/4 teaspoon soda
1/2 teaspoon salt
1 teaspoon cinnamon
1/4 teaspoon nutmeg
3/4 cup shortening

1 1/3 cups brown sugar, firmly packed
2 eggs
1 teaspoon vanilla
2 cups oats
1 cup nuts or raisins (optional)

Sift together flour, soda, salt, cinnamon, and nutmeg. Add shortening, brown sugar, eggs, and vanilla. Beat until smooth, about 2 minutes. Stir in oats and nuts or raisins, if desired. Drop by heaping teaspoonfuls onto greased cookie sheet. Bake at 350 degrees for 12 minutes.

"Tastes great!"

Ruth Schletewitz   **Roosevelt Jr. High School, Kingsburg**

COCONUT MACAROONS

Makes 2 to 3 dozen

1 1/3 cups coconut
1/3 cup sugar
2 tablespoons flour

1/8 teaspoon salt
2 egg whites
1/2 teaspoon almond extract

Mix all the ingredients together. Drop by teaspoonfuls on a greased and floured cookie sheet. Bake at 325 degrees for 20 to 30 minutes.

"This easy recipe makes delicious macaroons."

Bonnie Landin   **Garden Grove High School, Garden Grove**

ALMOND BARK COOKIES

Makes 99+

2 lbs. almond bark
1 cup peanut butter
3 cups Captain Crunch cereal

2 cups Rice Crispies cereal
3 cups salted peanuts
2 1/2 cups mini marshmallows

In heavy skillet or double boiler, melt almond bark slowly. Mix in peanut butter till creamy. Combine remaining ingredients in large bowl. Add bark mixture and mix well. Drop by large spoonfuls onto waxed paper. Set at room temperature for 30 minutes. Put into a container with pieces of waxed paper between layers. Refrigerate.

"This is a definite sweet tooth pleaser! Yummy!"

Cathy Miller   **Montclair High School, Montclair**

GRANDMA JACKIE'S M & M'S

Makes 36 cookies

½ cup margarine
1 cup sugar
1 egg
1 teaspoon vanilla

1½ cups flour, sifted
½ teaspoon baking soda
½ teaspoon salt
6 oz. M & M's

Cream margarine and sugar till soft. Add egg and vanilla; beat thoroughly. Sift dry ingredients together. Slowly add dry ingredients to sugar mixture. Stir in M&M's. Drop by spoonfuls on ungreased cookie sheet. Bake at 350 degrees for 8 to 10 minutes.

"The grandkids (and the big "kids") will pout for hours when they come to Grandma's and the cookie jar isn't filled with these. Dough refrigerates well, if it survives raiding, and can be baked later."

Jackie Rupp   **Home Street Middle School, Bishop**

CHRISTMAS CRISPIES

Makes 6 dozen

2½ cups flour, sifted
1 teaspoon baking soda
½ teaspoon salt
2 cubes butter
2 cups sugar
2 eggs

2 teaspoons vanilla
1 package (12 oz.) chocolate chips
2 cups nuts, chopped
2 cups rice krispies

Preheat oven to 350 degrees. Sift together flour, baking soda, and salt; set aside. Combine butter and sugar in a large bowl. Beat until creamy. Add eggs and vanilla. Gradually add the flour mixture and mix well. Add chocolate chips, nuts, and rice krispies. Drop by teaspoonfuls on lightly greased baking sheet. Bake at 350 degrees for 12 to 15 minutes.

"My relatives have made these cookies a tradition during the Christmas holidays."

June Muraoka   **Cypress High School, Cypress**

WHITE CHOCOLATE MACADAMIA NUT COOKIES

Makes about 18 cookies

½ cup butter
½ cup sugar
½ cup brown sugar
1 large egg
1 teaspoon vanilla
1¼ cups flour

½ teaspoon baking soda
½ teaspoon salt
¾ cup macadamia nuts
  (not chopped)
1 cup white chocolate chips

Mix butter with sugars until lumps are gone. Add ingredients in following order: egg, vanilla, flour, baking soda, and salt. Mix until creamy. Stir in macadamia nuts and white chocolate chips. For 18 large cookies, use a one-ounce ice cream scooper to drop cookies or roll into size of large walnuts. Bake at 375 degrees for 10 to 15 minutes.

"So-o-o-o good!"

Robin Ali-Christie   **Nevada Union High School, Grass Valley**

TRIPLE CHOCOLATE COOKIES

Makes 22 cookies

⅔ cup butter
⅔ cup sugar
⅓ cup brown sugar, packed
1 egg
1 teaspoon vanilla
2 ounces unsweetened chocolate,
  melted

1½ cups flour
1½ bars (3 oz. each) swiss dark
  chocolate, chopped
1 bar (3 oz.) white chocolate,
  chopped

Heat oven to 325 degrees. Lightly grease 2 cookie sheets. In large bowl, beat butter, sugars, egg, vanilla, and melted chocolate at medium high speed until fluffy. Reduce mixer speed to low, and add flour. Increase mixer speed gradually and beat just until blended. Stir in dark and white chocolate. Drop heaping tablespoonfuls of dough 2½" apart onto sheets. Bake for 17 minutes, or until tops look dry (bake 1 sheet at a time). Cool on sheet, about 5 minutes.

Brenda Umbro   **San Pasqual High School, Escondido**

JERI'S WORLD FAMOUS CHOCOLATE CHIP COOKIES

Makes 24 large cookies

⅓ cup shortening
⅓ cup butter (not margarine)
½ cup sugar
½ cup brown sugar
1 egg
1 teaspoon vanilla

1½ cups flour
½ teaspoon baking soda
½ teaspoon salt
½ cup nuts (optional)
1 cup chocolate chips
  (I use milk chocolate)

Mix the first 6 ingredients together well, then add the last 5. Drop dough with a cookie scoop or large tablespoon (should be the size of a golf ball). For a chewy cookie, bake at 375 degrees for 8 to 10 minutes. For a crisp cookie, bake for 10 to 12 minutes.

"These are really good, but not calorie free! Best if eaten immediately, the rest can be frozen."

Jeri Drake Lane　　　　　　**Canyon Springs High School, Moreno Valley**

CHEWY CHOCOLATE COOKIES

Makes 4 to 5 dozen

1¼ cups butter, softened	*1 teaspoon baking soda*
2 cups sugar	*½ teaspoon salt*
2 eggs	*1 package (12 oz.) peanut butter*
2 teaspoon vanilla	*chips or semisweet chocolate*
2 cups flour	*chips*
¾ cup Hershey's Cocoa	

Heat oven to 350 degrees. In a large mixing bowl, cream butter and sugar until light and fluffy. Add eggs and vanilla; beat well. Combine flour, cocoa, baking soda, and salt; gradually blend into creamed mixture. Stir in peanut butter or chocolate chips. Drop by teaspoonfuls onto ungreased cookie sheet. Bake for 8 to 9 minutes. (Do not overbake; cookies will be soft. They will puff while baking and flatten while cooling.)

"One of my kid's favorite cookies. These never last long."

Cari Sheridan　　　　　　　**Grace Yokley School, Ontario**

CRY BABIES

Makes about 4 dozen

2 cups flour	*½ cup milk*
1 teaspoon soda	*¼ cup molasses*
1 teaspoon cinnamon	*1 teaspoon vanilla*
1 teaspoon nutmeg	*2 cups oats*
½ teaspoon salt	*½ cup raisins*
⅔ cup shortening	*½ cup walnuts*
⅔ cup sugar	*1 cup chocolate chips*
1 egg	

Preheat oven to 350 degrees. Sift together first 5 ingredients and set aside. Cream together shortening and sugar. Stir in egg, milk, molasses, vanilla. Add remaining ingredients and mix thoroughly. Drop by teaspoonfuls onto ungreased cookie sheets. Bake for 15 minutes and remove to cooling rack. Store in airtight containers.

"Mom used to make these!"

Maria Fregulia　　　　　　**Lassen Union High School, Susanville**

MICHELE'S CHOCOLATE CHIP COOKIES

Makes 8 dozen

½ cup (1 stick) butter
½ cup (1 stick) margarine
1 cup light brown sugar, firmly
  packed
1 cup sugar
1 egg
1 tablespoon milk
2 teaspoons vanilla

3½ cups flour, sifted
1 teaspoon baking soda
1 teaspoon salt
1 cup vegetable oil
1 cup cornflakes
1 cup quick oats
1 package (12 oz.) semisweet
  chocolate chips

In a large bowl, cream together the butter, margarine, and sugars. When smooth, stir in the egg, milk, and vanilla. Sift flour, baking soda, and salt onto wax paper. Stir flour mixture into creamed mixture, alternately with oil, until mixture is thoroughly combined. Stir in cornflakes, oats, and chocolate chips. Drop by teaspoonfuls onto greased cookie sheet. Bake at 350 degrees for 12 minutes or until golden brown.

"My students tried lots of chocolate chip cookie recipes, and this is the best! It was given to me by Michelle O'Connor, a friend in my jazzercise class. The cookies are crisp and delicious."

Judy Conner   **Santa Ana Valley High School, Santa Ana**

LION DEN COOKIES

Makes about 4 dozen

½ cup shortening
½ cup butter
2½ cups flour
1 cup brown sugar, packed
½ cup sugar
2 eggs
1 teaspoon vanilla

1 teaspoon ground cinnamon
½ teaspoon baking soda
1 package (6 oz.) butterscotch
  chips
1 package (6 oz.) white chocolate
  chips
1 cup pecans

In a mixing bowl, beat shortening and butter with electric mixer for 30 seconds. Add about half the flour, the brown sugar, sugar, eggs, vanilla, cinnamon, and baking soda. Beat mixture till thoroughly combined. Beat in remaining flour. Stir in butterscotch and white chocolate chips. Stir in nuts. Drop dough by round teaspoonfuls 2" apart on ungreased cookie sheet. Bake at 375 degrees for 8 to 10 minutes. Cool on cookie rack.

"Our classes looked for a recipe that reminded them of our mascot. White chocolate for the sharp teeth and butterscotch for the shaggy mane color."

Stephanie Zupanovich   **Kerman High School, Kerman**

MINT COOKIES

Makes about 3 dozen

2 egg whites
1/8 teaspoon cream of tartar
pinch salt
1/4 teaspoon lemon juice

1/4 teaspoon vanilla
3/4 cup sugar
1 package (10 oz.) mint morsels

Preheat oven to 350 degrees. Beat egg whites, cream of tartar, and salt until stiff. Add lemon juice and vanilla. Next, add sugar gradually; beat until very stiff. Fold in chips. **Turn off oven**. Drop by teaspoonfuls onto brown paper bags which are cut to fit cookie sheets. Place cookies in oven and leave overnight.

"Very light tasting cookie."

Diane Castro   **Quartz Hill High School, Lancaster**

LEMONADE COOKIES

1 cup margarine
1 cup sugar
2 eggs
3 to 3½ cups flour (depends on
thickness of lemonade)

1 teaspoon soda
1 can (6 oz.) frozen lemonade
sugar to sprinkle

Cream margarine and sugar; add eggs and beat. Add flour and soda alternately with ½ cup lemonade. Drop onto cookie sheet and bake at 400 degrees about 8 minutes. Brush hot cookies lightly with remaining lemonade and sprinkle with sugar. (This task is easier if you put the sugar in a salt shaker.)

"A treat that is sweet and tart at the same time."

Gloria King   **Schurr High School, Montebello**

CHEWY LEMON COOKIES

Makes 4 dozen

1 package lemon cake mix
4 to 5 ounces Cool Whip

1 egg
powdered sugar

Mix together the cake mix, Cool Whip, and egg. Drop by teaspoonfuls into powdered sugar. Place on greased cookie sheet. Bake at 350 degrees for 8 to 10 minutes.

"Super easy for those last minute PTA meetings."

Sonja Tyree   **Ruben Ayala High School, Chino**

MARY ANNE'S CHOCOLATE YOGURT MELTS

Makes 4 dozen

1 package devils food cake mix
1 package (8 oz.) cherry yogurt
1 egg

2 tablespoons butter, melted
2/3 cup walnuts, chopped
1 package (6 oz.) chocolate chips

Combine cake mix, yogurt, egg, and butter. Beat until well blended. Stir in walnuts and chocolate chips. Drop dough by teaspoonfuls 2 inches apart on ungreased cookie sheet. Bake at 350 degrees for 12 to 15 minutes. Cool on wire rack.

"Quick, easy, and a chocolate lover's delight!"

Sharon Kleven   **San Gabriel High School, San Gabriel**

CARROT BARS

Serves a group

4 eggs
2 cups sugar
1½ cups oil
2 teaspoons vanilla
4 small jars baby food carrots
2½ cups flour
2 teaspoons baking soda
1 teaspoon cinnamon

1 teaspoon salt
2 cups walnuts, chopped
Frosting:
1 package (8 oz.) cream cheese
1 cube margarine
1 teaspoon vanilla
1 box powdered sugar

Mix eggs, sugar, and oil; beat well. Add carrots and vanilla. Mix dry ingredients together and add to first mixture. Add chopped nuts. Pour into greased and floured jelly roll pan or cookie sheet with sides. Bake at 350 degrees for about 30 minutes.
Frosting: Combine the cream cheese, margarine, vanilla, and powdered sugar; beat well. Spread on cooled baked mixture. Cut into bars and serve.

Cheryle Apple   **Rio Vista High School, Rio Vista**

DATE NUT BARS

Makes about 2 dozen

3 cups dates (1 lb.), diced
1 cup water
½ cup sugar
½ cup nuts, chopped
¾ cup butter

1 cup brown sugar
1¼ cups flour
1 teaspoon salt
1¼ cups quick oats

Combine dates, water, and sugar in a saucepan. Boil for 5 minutes or until thickened. Cool slightly. Add nuts and set aside. Cream butter. Gradually add brown sugar and beat until light and fluffy. Add flour, salt, and oats. Mix until well blended (mixture will be crumbly). Pack two-thirds of the mixture evenly and firmly on the bottom of a greased 13 x 9" baking pan. Spread with the date mixture. Sprinkle with remaining crumb mixture. Bake at 350 degrees for 30 minutes. Cool and cut into squares.

"These bars are wonderful with a cup of coffee and some conversation."

Cynthia Hoiland   **Mojave High School, Mojave**

PUMPKIN BARS

Makes 24 bars

4 eggs
1¾ cups sugar
1 cup oil
1 can (16 oz.) pumpkin
2 cups flour
2 teaspoons baking powder
2 teaspoons cinnamon
1 teaspoon salt

1 teaspoon soda
1 cup nuts, chopped
Frosting:
1 package (3 oz.) cream cheese,
  softened
⅓ cup butter
1 teaspoon vanilla
2 cups powdered sugar

Combine eggs, sugar, oil, and pumpkin and beat until fluffy. Add dry ingredients and mix thoroughly. Add nuts and mix well. Place in an ungreased 15 x 10 x 1" pan. Bake at 350 degrees for 25 to 30 minutes. Cool. Mix all ingredients for frosting and spread mixture on cooled bars.

Sally Oxford   **Monache High School, Porterville**

SUE'S LEMON BARS

Makes 16 bars

1 coconut pecan frosting mix
⅔ cup butter, softened
1 cup flour

1 teaspoon baking powder
1 can sweetened condensed milk
½ cup lemon juice

Mix dry frosting mix, butter, flour, and baking powder. Press half of this mixture into an 8" square baking dish. Beat together sweetened condensed milk and lemon juice. Pour on top of crust. Sprinkle remainder of frosting mixture on top of filling. Bake at 350 degrees for 30 to 40 minutes or until lightly browned.

"This can easily be doubled and prepared in a 9 x 13" pan. They won't last long--too delicious!"

Sue Nall   **Temple City High School, Temple City**

GOOEY CARAMEL BROWNIES

Makes 2 dozen

50 caramels
2/3 cup evaporated milk
1 package German chocolate
  cake mix

12 ounces chocolate chips
1 cup walnuts, chopped
3/4 cup butter, melted

Unwrap caramels and melt in top of double boiler with 1/3 cup of the evaporated milk; set aside. Mix together the cake mix, remaining 1/3 cup evaporated milk, 1 cup of the chocolate chips, nuts, and melted butter. Mix until dough holds together. Press half of dough into greased and floured 9 x 13" baking pan. Bake at 350 degrees for 6 minutes. Remove from oven. Spread caramel mixture over the top. Sprinkle with remaining chocolate chips. Put the remaining half of dough on top. Return to oven and bake an additional 15 to 18 minutes. Cool; refrigerate for 30 minutes; cut into bars.

"Save at least half of dough for top layer. The most difficult part of this recipe is unwrapping the caramels!"

Diedre Simon   **Norwalk High School, Norwalk**

DOUBLE DECKER CONFETTI BROWNIES

Makes 24 bars

3/4 cup butter or margarine,
  softened
1 cup sugar
1 cup brown sugar
1 teaspoon vanilla
3 eggs
2 1/2 cups flour

2 1/2 teaspoons baking powder
1/4 teaspoon salt
1/3 cup unsweetened cocoa
1 tablespoon butter or
  margarine, melted
3/4 cup M & M's plain chocolate
  candies

Beat softened butter or margarine and sugars until fluffy; beat in vanilla and eggs. Stir in 2 1/4 cups flour mixed with baking powder and salt, mixing well. Divide batter in half. Into half of the batter, stir in cocoa and melted butter. Spread into greased 13 x 9" pan. Into remaining batter, stir in remaining flour; fold in 1/2 cup plain candies. Spread evenly over chocolate layer. Bake at 350 degrees for 20 minutes. Sprinkle with remaining candies; pressing in slightly. Bake an additional 15 minutes or until edges are lightly browned. Remove to wire rack to cool.

M & M Mars Company   **Accomac, Virginia**

HURRY UP MICROWAVE BROWNIES

Makes 16 bars

1/2 cup margarine
1/2 cup cocoa
1 cup sugar
3/4 cup flour
1/2 teaspoon baking powder

1/2 teaspoon salt
2 eggs
1/2 cup chocolate chips
1/2 cup nuts, chopped

Melt margarine and cocoa in the microwave. Stir in the sugar, flour, baking powder, salt, and eggs. Stir in chocolate chips and nuts. Place baking dish (I use a 9" glass round cake pan) on top of a custard cup in the microwave, to allow the rays to penetrate through the brownies. Bake on 50% power for 10 minutes, turning ¼ turn about every 2 minutes.

"A quick, easy family favorite!"

Laurie Owen   **Hoover High School, San Diego**

ONE-PAN BROWNIES

Makes 36 bars

½ cup margarine or butter	*½ cup flour*
2 squares bitter chocolate	*1 teaspoon vanilla*
1 cup sugar	*½ to 1 cup nuts, chopped*
2 eggs	

Melt the margarine in a double boiler. Remove pan from heat and, using pan as a mixing bowl, add the sugar gradually. Beat 2 eggs and add to mixture; stir and mix well. Add the flour and vanilla. Combine well. Add nuts. Pour into a greased and floured 8" square pan. Bake at 350 degrees for 25 to 30 minutes.

"Only one pan to wash."

Adrienne Steele   **Lee Jr. High School, Woodland**

TRI-LEVEL BROWNIES

Makes 24 to 30 bars

Layer 1:
¾ cup flour
⅜ teaspoon salt
⅜ teaspoon baking soda
1½ cups rolled oats, uncooked
¾ cup brown sugar
9 tablespoons butter, melted
Layer 3:
1 square unsweetened chocolate
3 tablespoons butter
1½ to 2 cups powdered sugar,
   sifted
1 teaspoon vanilla
2 tablespoons hot water

Layer 2:
1½ squares unsweetened
   chocolate
6 tablespoons butter
¾ cup sugar
2 eggs
1⅓ cups flour
⅜ teaspoon salt
⅜ teaspoon baking powder
6 tablespoons milk
⅜ teaspoon vanilla
½ cup nuts, chopped (optional)

Layer 1: Mix together flour, salt, baking soda, oats, brown sugar, and melted butter. Pat evenly into a 9 x 13" sheet pan. Bake in preheated 350 degrees oven for 10 minutes.

Layer 2: Melt chocolate and butter. Add sugar and eggs and blend completely. In a separate bowl, mix flour, salt, and baking powder. In a measuring cup place the 6 tablespoons milk and vanilla. Alternating the milk/vanilla mixture with the dry ingredients, and add to the chocolate/egg mixture. Fold in nuts. Spread batter over baked layer. Bake at 350 degrees for 25 minutes.

Layer 3 (Frosting): Melt chocolate and butter. Remove from heat and add sifted powdered sugar and vanilla. Blend in 2 tablespoons hot water if needed. Spread over cooled brownies.

"This was a family favorite when I was growing up."

Donna A. Small   **Santana High School, Santee**

PEPPERMINT BROWNIES

Makes lots

2 eggs	*½ cup oil*
½ cup buttermilk	*4 tablespoons cocoa*
¼ teaspoon cinnamon	**Topping:**
dash of salt	*8 tablespoons butter*
2 cups sugar	*4 cups powdered sugar*
2 cups flour	*4 tablespoons cream*
1 teaspoon baking soda	*1 teaspoon peppermint flavoring*
1 teaspoon vanilla	*few drops green food coloring*
1 stick margarine	*4 squares semisweet chocolate*
1 cup water	*4 tablespoons butter, melted*

Beat together first 4 ingredients. Add sugar, flour, soda, and vanilla. Bring to a boil the margarine, water, oil, and cocoa. Add to first mixture. Put in one 18 x 12 x 1" pan **or** one 13 x 9 x 2" **and** two 8 x 6 x 2" pans. Bake at 400 degrees for 20 minutes or until done to touch.

Topping: Mix butter, powdered sugar, cream, peppermint flavoring, and green food coloring. Mix until creamy and spread on cooled brownies. Refrigerate after topping. Melt together semisweet chocolate and melted butter. Cool slightly to prevent melting of peppermint layer. Spread quickly and evenly on peppermint frosting. Chill partially and then cut in desired pieces. Store in refrigerator until ready to use (or may be frozen).

"This recipe is sinfully rich, but oh so good!"

Libby Bruce   **Troy High School, Fullerton**

"SNICKER" BROWNIES

Makes 24 to 30 bars

14 ounces Kraft caramels	*¾ cup butter, melted*
⅔ cup evaporated milk, divided	*1 cup unsalted nuts, chopped*
1 package German Chocolate cake mix	*6 ounces chocolate chips*

Melt caramels with ⅓ cup evaporated milk. Set aside; cool. Mix cake mix, butter, ⅓ cup evaporated milk, and nuts. Spread half of mixture into 9 x 13" greased pan. Bake at 350 degrees for 6 minutes. Spread chocolate chips over mixture in pan. Spread melted caramel over mixture in pan. Crumble remaining mixture over all. Bake at 350 degrees for 15 minutes.

"This was given to me by a mother who was doing a demonstration for my class."

Darlene Haws   **Highland High School, Bakersfield**

CALIFORNIA CHOCOLATE BARS

Makes about 16 bars

½ cup sugar
6 tablespoons butter or
  margarine, softened
¼ cup light brown sugar, packed
1 egg
1 teaspoon orange peel, grated
1 teaspoon vanilla
1 cup flour

½ teaspoon baking soda
¼ teaspoon salt
½ cup dried apricots, chopped
½ cup walnuts, coarsely chopped
1 cup premium milk chocolate
  chunks
Milk Chocolate Glaze (recipe
  follows)

Heat oven to 350 degrees. Grease 9" square pan. In large mixer bowl, beat sugar, butter, brown sugar, and egg until light and fluffy. Add orange peel and vanilla; blend well. Combine flour, baking soda, and salt; add to butter mixture. Stir in apricots, walnuts, and chocolate chunks; spread into prepared pan. Bake 25 to 30 minutes or until lightly browned and bars begin to pull away from sides of pan. Cool completely. Prepare Milk Chocolate Glaze; drizzle over top. Allow to set; cut into bars.
Milk Chocolate Glaze: In small microwave-safe bowl, place ¾ cup premium milk chocolate chunks and 2 tablespoons shortening. Microwave at 100% high for 45 seconds or until melted and smooth when stirred.

Hershey Foods Corporation   **Hershey, Pennsylvania**

PEANUT CRISP BAR

Makes 4 dozen

½ cup sugar
½ cup light corn syrup
dash of salt
1 cup peanut butter
2 cups crisp rice cereal

¼ cup margarine
¼ cup brown sugar, packed
1 tablespoon milk
½ teaspoon vanilla
1¼ cups powdered sugar, sifted

Combine sugar, corn syrup, and salt. Cook and stir till sugar is dissolved. Blend in peanut butter and stir in cereal. Pat evenly in 11 x 7" foil-lined pan. In a small saucepan, melt margarine and brown sugar. Remove from heat. Add milk and vanilla. Stir in powdered sugar and beat smooth. Remove cereal mixture from pan. Spread top with frosting. Chill. Cut into small bars.

Margaret Hodge   **Grace Davis High School, Modesto**

CARAMEL OATMEAL CHEWIES

Makes 32

1¾ cups Quaker Oats (quick or
    old fashioned)
1½ cups flour
¾ cup brown sugar
½ teaspoon baking soda
¼ teaspoon salt (optional)

¾ cup margarine, melted
1 cup nuts, chopped
1 package (6 oz.) chocolate chips
1 bag (14 oz.) vanilla caramels
¼ cup water

Preheat oven to 350 degrees. Grease 9 x 13" pan. Combine first 5 ingredients. Add margarine and mix until crumbly; reserve 1 cup for topping. Press remaining mixture into pan. Bake 10 minutes and then cool. Top with chopped nuts and chocolate. In a medium saucepan, melt caramels with water over low heat. Stir until smooth and remove from heat. Drizzle over chocolate to within ¼" of pan edges. Sprinkle with reserved oat mixture. Bake 15 to 18 minutes more. Cool until chocolate is set. Cut into 32 bars.

"I got this delicious recipe from one of my students, Dana MacIntyre."

Kelly Goughnour   **San Luis Obispo High School, San Luis Obispo**

FROSTED SCOTCH BARS

Makes 24 bars

1 cup shortening
½ cup sugar
½ cup brown sugar
1 egg
1 teaspoon vanilla

1 cup flour
¼ teaspoon salt
1 cup rolled oats
1 package (6 oz.) chocolate chips
1 cup nuts, chopped

Cream together shortening and sugars. Add egg and vanilla to creamed mixture. Add flour, salt, and rolled oats; mix well. Spread into a greased 10 x 16" pan with sides. Bake at 350 degrees for 25 minutes. Remove from oven; spread chocolate chips on top. Return to oven until chips are melted. Remove from oven and sprinkle nuts on top. Cool completely.

"This has been a family favorite for years and it's so quick and easy to make."

Cindy Johnson   **Orland High School, Orland**

TOFFEE BARS

Makes 16 bars

1 cup brown sugar, firmly packed
1 cup (2 sticks) butter, melted
2 cups flour, sifted

1 teaspoon vanilla
¼ cup nuts, **or** ¼ cup raisins, **or**
¼ cup chocolate chips

Combine melted butter, brown sugar, and vanilla. Add sifted flour gradually, and stir until well mixed (mixture will become fairly stiff). Stir in nuts, raisins, or chocolate chips. Spread mixture into an ungreased 8" square pan. Bake at 350 degrees for 25 to 30 minutes. Cool and cut into 2 inch squares while still slightly warm.

"For real tasty and delicious toffee bars, use raisins, nuts, AND chocolate chips."

Lenora Dugas   **Hoover Jr. High School, Lakewood**

DOUBLE C'S BARS

Makes 36 bars

1¼ cups flour
½ cup powdered sugar
½ cup cold butter or margarine,
cut into 6 pieces
14 oz. caramels (I use 1 pkg.
 peanut chips)
⅓ cup evaporated milk

¼ cup butter
6 oz. chocolate chips
3 tablespoons shortening
 (Crisco)
¾ cup peanuts or ¾ cup Heath
Bar or ¾ cup rice crispies

Mix flour, powdered sugar, and butter until crumbly. Lightly press into an ungreased 9 x 13" pan. Bake at 350 degrees for 10 to 12 minutes or lightly brown. Using a heavy pan, melt caramels or chips, evaporated milk, and butter over low heat, stirring constantly. Spread over baked crust.
Using a medium saucepan, melt chocolate chips and shortening over low heat, stirring frequently. Remove from heat and stir in either the peanuts, Heath brickle, or rice crispies. Carefully spread over the filling. Cool completely and cut.

Marie Coots   **Huntington Beach High School, Huntington Beach**

SURFER SQUARES

Makes 24

1 package (6 oz.) butterscotch
 pieces
¼ cup brown sugar
¼ cup butter
1 egg
¾ cup flour

1 teaspoon baking powder
1 teaspoon salt
1 cup semisweet chocolate pieces
1 cup mini marshmallows
½ cup walnuts, chopped
1 teaspoon vanilla

Grease an 8" square cake pan. Melt butterscotch pieces, sugar, and butter over low heat. Add egg; beat well. Mix in flour, baking powder, and salt. Stir in remaining ingredients. Spread into pan. Bake at 350 degrees for 20 to 25 minutes.

Pat Smith   **Kern Valley High School, Lake Isabella**

BUTTER PECAN TURTLE COOKIES

Makes 3 to 4 dozen bars

Crust:
2 cups flour
1 cup brown sugar
½ cup butter, softened
1 cup whole pecan halves

Caramel Layer:
⅔ cup butter
½ cup brown sugar
1 cup chocolate chips

Crust: Combine crust ingredients, except pecan halves. Mix at medium speed 2 to 3 minutes or until well mixed and particles are fine. Pat evenly and firmly into greased 13 x 9" pan. Sprinkle pecans evenly over unbaked crust. Set aside.

Caramel layer: Combine ⅔ cup butter and brown sugar in 1 quart saucepan. Cook over medium heat, stirring at all times until mixture begins to boil. Boil ½ to 1 minute. Pour caramel mixture over pecans and crust. Bake at 350 degrees for 18 minutes, or until entire caramel layer is bubbly and crust is golden brown.

Remove from oven and immediately sprinkle with chips. Allow chips to melt slightly (2 to 3 minutes). Slightly swirl chips as they melt, leaving some whole for a marbled effect. Do not spread! Cool completely and cut into bars.

"These rich bar cookies are a favorite at any time of year. They are delicious!"

Karen Bennett   **Norco High School, Norco**

CHOCOLATE CARAMEL BARS

Makes 36 bars

1 package German chocolate
  cake mix
½ cup butter, softened
1 egg
½ cup butter
½ cup evaporated milk

1 package (14 oz.) caramels
½ cup nuts, chopped
½ cup chocolate ready-to-spread
  frosting
3 to 4 teaspoons water

Preheat oven to 350 degrees. Mix dry cake mix, softened butter, and egg until crumbly; reserve 1½ cups of this mixture. Press remaining crumbly mixture in an ungreased 13 x 9" pan. Bake until crust appears dry for 10 to 12 minutes. Cool for 10 minutes.

Heat butter, milk, and caramels over low heat, stirring occasionally, until caramels are melted. Pour over crust; sprinkle with nuts and reserved crumbly mixture. Bake for 25 to 30 minutes. Cool.

Mix frosting and water, 1 teaspoon at a time until thin enough to drizzle over the bars. Drizzle and then loosen edges of bars with spatula. Refrigerate until caramel mixture becomes firm, about 1 hour. Cut into 36 bars.

"These bars are yummy! You won't be able to stop with just one!"

Carole Delap   **Golden West High School, Visalia**

CHOCOLATE BARS

Makes about 24 bars

½ cup (1 stick) margarine
½ cup Crisco
¼ cup cocoa
½ teaspoon salt
1 cup water
2 cups flour
1 teaspoon soda
2 cups sugar
½ cup buttermilk

2 eggs
1 teaspoon vanilla
Frosting:
½ cup margarine
¼ cup cocoa
⅓ cup buttermilk
1 pound powdered sugar
1 teaspoon vanilla

In a heavy saucepan, combine the margarine, Crisco, cocoa, salt, and water to a boil. In a separate bowl, combine flour soda, sugar, buttermilk, eggs, and vanilla. Add to first mixture and mix well. Pour into a greased 11 x 16" cookie pan and bake at 350 degrees for 20 minutes.
Frosting: In a saucepan, boil the margarine, cocoa, and buttermilk. Add the sugar and vanilla and mix well. Pour over the bars while they are still hot.

"Simple and good."

Patsy L. Jones   **DeAnza Middle School, Ventura**

NUT TORTES

Makes 32 bars

10 eggs
1½ cups sugar
¾ pound walnuts or hazelnuts

1 tablespoon orange peel, grated
1 package (8 oz.) Baker's
  semisweet chocolate

Grind the nuts. Separate the eggs. Beat egg whites till stiff peaks form. Beat egg yolk and sugar till thick and lemony color. Fold egg whites into egg yolks. Fold in nuts and orange peel. Pour batter into 13 x 9" baking pan lined with wax paper. Bake at 350 degrees for 1 hour. Let cool. Melt chocolate and spread onto cooled cake. Cut into squares.

Astrid Curfman   **Rogers Jr. High School, Long Beach**

WALNUT SLICE BARS

Makes 72 bars

2 cubes butter
½ cup sugar
2 cups plus 4 tablespoons flour
½ cup cornstarch
4 eggs
1 package brown sugar
½ teaspoon baking powder
2 teaspoons vanilla

2 cups walnuts, chopped
1 package (8 oz.) coconut, flaked
Frosting:
1 cube butter
1 box powdered sugar
1 package (4 oz.) cream cheese
juice of 1 lemon

Cream butter and sugar. Sift together and add the 2 cups flour and cornstarch. Mix thoroughly (knead if possible). Spread or press into bottom of 11 x 17" jelly roll pan. Bake at 300 degrees for 15 minutes. Beat eggs and brown sugar until very light. Add the 4 tablespoons flour, baking powder, and vanilla; beat. Add walnuts and coconut; beat. Spread over shortbread mixture. Increase oven to 350 degrees and bake for 20 minutes. Cool completely.

Frosting: Beat together cube of butter, powdered sugar, cream cheese, and lemon juice. Spread frosting and cut into 72 bars.

"This recipe is great when you need to serve many people. Great for teas and fashion shows."

Betty Wells   **Oroville High School, Oroville**

Refrigerated Goodies

HEAVENLY CHOCOLATE SUNDAE CUPS

Serves 4

*1 cup (½ pint) whipping cream,
chilled
½ cup chocolate syrup, chilled
1 tablespoon Amaretto di
Saronno liqueur
½ cup toasted almonds, finely
chopped*

*1 pint Baskin Robbins Chocolate
Mousse Royale ice cream
Chocolate Sauce (below)
¼ cup toasted almonds, coarsely
chopped or sliced
stemmed maraschino cherries*

Combine whipping cream and chocolate syrup in a mixing bowl. Beat until mixture holds its shape. Fold in Amaretto and almonds. Divide into four mounded portions on a wax paper-lined baking sheet, or in a saucer, champagne, or sherbet glasses. Using the back of a spoon, make a depression in the center of each; mound large enough for a scoop of ice cream. Freeze until firm, about 2 or 3 hours. Place a scoop of ice cream in each chocolate cream cup and return to the freezer. To serve, pour warm sauce over ice cream in cups. Sprinkle with ¼ cup toasted almonds and garnish with maraschino cherries.

Chocolate Sauce: Melt 2 tablespoons butter in a saucepan over low heat. Remove from heat and stir in ½ cup sugar and 3 tablespoons unsweetened cocoa. Add 6 tablespoons half and half, blending well. Cook over low heat, stirring constantly, until mixture just begins to boil. Remove from heat and stir in 1 tablespoon Amaretto. Cool slightly. Or, warm ⅔ cup (5-oz. pouch) Baskin Robbins Hot Fudge Topping, remove from heat, and stir in 1 tablespoon Amaretto.

Mary King - Cover Photo   Baskin Robbins Show Off Recipe Prize Winner

TERRIFIC STRAWBERRY SODA

Serves 1

*2 tablespoons strawberry jam
2 tablespoons sweetened
whipped cream
2 tablespoons club soda, chilled*

*1 scoop Baskin Robbins
strawberry ice cream
club soda to fill glass, chilled
1 lemon slice*

In a tall tumbler, place strawberry jam, whipped cream, and club soda, and beat together with a long-handled spoon. Add ice cream. Add chilled soda to fill the glass and give the whole thing a gentle stir. Perch a lemon slice on the rim of the glass.

Baskin Robbins   **Glendale, California**

NEW YORK CHOCOLATE EGG CREAM

Serves 1

¼ cup chocolate flavored syrup
¼ cup light cream

½ cup chilled ginger ale or club
soda, freshly opened

All ingredients should be cold. Measure syrup into tall glass; stir in cream to blend. Slowly pour ginger ale or club soda down side of glass, stirring constantly. Serve immediately.

Hershey Foods Corporation   **Hershey, Pennsylvania**

CAPPUCCINO COOLER

Serves 4

1½ cups cold coffee
1½ cups vanilla ice cream

⅓ cup chocolate flavored syrup
crushed ice
fresh fruit (optional)

In blender place coffee, ice cream, and syrup. Cover; blend until smooth. Serve immediately over crushed ice; garnish with fresh fruit, if desired.

Hershey Foods Corporation   **Hershey, Pennsylvania**

BANANAS FOSTER

Serves 2

2 tablespoons butter
1 large or 2 small bananas
¼ cup light brown sugar, packed
dash of nutmeg or cinnamon
¼ teaspoon orange peel, grated

2 tablespoons banana liqueur,
if desired
¼ cup rum
2 large scoops vanilla ice cream
toasted almonds, slivered or
sliced

Melt butter in skillet. Slice or halve the bananas lengthwise. When butter froths, add bananas. Cook until lightly browned. Add next 4 ingredients along with 2 tablespoons rum. Stir until blended. Boil until syrupy. Place ice cream in two heat-proof dishes. Warm remaining 2 tablespoons rum in small long-handled pot. Ignite with long match. Pour over bananas. Spoon bananas and sauce over ice cream. Top with almonds.

"This is a wonderful ending to a candlelight dinner for two! Connie Way from Ball Jr. High School gave me this recipe."

Marianne Traw   **Ball Jr. High School, Anaheim**

PELE'S BANANAS

Serves 4 to 6

4 tablespoons butter
6 tablespoons brown sugar
1 teaspoon cinnamon
4 bananas, sliced

½ cup banana liqueur
½ cup rum
4 to 6 scoops vanilla ice cream

Melt butter over low heat in a flambe pan or large skillet. Add sugar and cinnamon and mix well. Saute bananas until they begin to turn soft. Add banana liqueur and half the rum and simmer. Bring remainder of rum to a boil in a separate saucepan. Quickly pour into flambe pan and ignite using a long match. When the flame dies, serve banana and sauce over ice cream.

"A delicious and impressive dessert to serve company."

Pat Hufnagel   **Esperanza High School, Anaheim**

NO COOK VANILLA ICE CREAM

3 cups sugar
1 teaspoon salt

4 teaspoons vanilla
3 quarts half and half

Dissolve sugar and salt in 1 quart of half and half in the freezing unit. Pour in the remaining ingredients. Churn in electric or hand crank ice cream freezer.

"If you use an electric or hand crank ice cream freezer frequently, you could save money by buying a 50 lb. sack of rock salt, such as is used in a water softening unit."

Sue Walters   **Morse High School, San Diego**

FROSTED CAFE AU LAIT

Serves 4

1 pint Baskin Robbins Jamoca
   ice cream
1 pint Baskin Robbins Chocolate
   Fudge ice cream

⅓ cup brandy (use more
   if you like)
¼ cup milk

In a blender, combine the slightly softened ice creams with the brandy and milk. Whir until just blended. Freeze for at least 3 hours. When serving, add whipped cream, chocolate curls, and a cherry.

Baskin Robbins   **Glendale, California**

Chocorange Torte, Page 5

Butterscotch Ring, Page 145

Double Decker Confetti Brownies, Page 80

Cherry Cheese Ring-Around, Page 147

BAKED ALASKA

12 servings

1 package devils food cake mix
1 quart brick chocolate chip
  ice cream

4 egg whites
½ teaspoon cream of tartar
⅔ cup brown sugar, packed

Preheat oven to 350 degrees. Mix cake according to package directions and bake in one 9" round pan and one 9" square pan. Bake round layer 30 to 35 minutes and square layer 25 to 30 minutes. (Freeze round layer for other use.)
Cover a baking sheet with aluminum foil. Place cooled square cake on baking sheet. Place ice cream on cake. Leaving 1" edge, trim cake with ice cream. Freeze cake and ice cream. Heat oven to 500 degrees. Beat egg whites and cream of tartar until foamy. Beat in brown sugar, 1 tablespoon at a time; continue beating until stiff and glossy. Completely cover cake and ice cream with meringue, sealing it to foil on baking sheet. (If desired, it can be frozen up to 24 hours at this point.) Bake on lowest rack in oven 3 to 5 minutes or until meringue is light brown. Trim foil to edge of meringue and transfer cake to serving plate. Cut into 6 slices and each slice in half. Serve immediately.

"Looks spectacular, but SO easy!"

Barbara Hansen   **Montclair High School, Montclair**

GRASSHOPPER PIE

Serves 6 to 8

3 tablespoons butter
18 crushed Oreo cookies
24 marshmallows
½ cup milk

¼ cup creme de menthe
2 tablespoons creme de cocoa
1 cup whipped cream, whipped

Melt butter; stir into crushed cookies. Press into 8" pie pan. In a double boiler, melt the marshmallows in the milk; stir in creme de menthe and creme de cocoa. Fold in whipped cream; pour into pie crust. Freeze until firm (several hours).

"Great company recipe. Can be made ahead and can be doubled."

Ginny Rocheleau   **Muirlands Jr. High School, La Jolla**

FANTASTIC FROZEN PEANUT BUTTER PIE

Serves 8 to 10

1 package (8 oz.) cream cheese,
  room temperature
1 cup powdered sugar
½ cup creamy peanut butter
½ cup milk
1 teaspoon vanilla

3 cups Cool Whip or 1½ cups
  whipped cream, whipped
9" chocolate wafer pie crust
½ cup peanuts, chopped
chocolate shavings

Beat cheese until fluffy. Add sugar gradually, beating until smooth. Add peanut butter, mixing well. Stir in milk; gradually add vanilla. Fold topping into creamed mixture. Pour into crumb crust. Sprinkle with chopped peanuts and garnish with chocolate shavings. Freeze at least 4 hours. Let stand 5 to 10 minutes at room temperature before cutting. (If frozen longer than 4 hours, allow 20 minutes before cutting.)

"You may use a graham cracker crust or garnish only with the chocolate and omit the peanuts on top."

Lucille Bell   **Palmdale High School, Palmdale**

HULA PIE

Serves 8

¼ cup butter or margarine, melted
¼ cup sugar
1½ cup chocolate cookie crumbs
1 quart macadamia nut ice cream

hot fudge topping, warmed
macadamia nuts, chopped
whipped cream
maraschino cherries

Mix first three ingredients and press into 9" pie plate to form crust. Bake at 300 degrees for 10 minutes. Cool. Pack macadamia nut ice cream on the crust. Freeze till firm. To serve, cut hula pie and garnish with warmed hot fudge topping, macadamia nuts, whipped cream, and cherries.

"My husband and I tasted Hula Pie on Maui. Soon after we returned home, I figured out this recipe and surprised him!"

Gail Hurt   **Estancia High School, Costa Mesa**

PUMPKIN SUNDAE PIE

Serves 8 to 10

1 quart vanilla ice cream
1 "prepared graham cracker pie crust
1 cup canned pumpkin
½ pint Cool Whip

1 cup sugar
½ teaspoon cinnamon
½ teaspoon salt
¼ teaspoon ginger
⅛ teaspoon cloves

Spread ice cream into crust about half full. Combine Cool Whip, pumpkin, sugar, and spices. Mix thoroughly. Pour over top of ice cream. Freeze 2 hours before serving.

"A great dessert to prepare ahead of time in November or December. Just set out of freezer 15 minutes before serving to slice easily."

Janet Rupp   **El Rancho Middle School, Anaheim**

LUSCIOUS LEMON LAYER TORTE

Serves 6 to 8

Crumb Crust:
1¾ cups graham cracker crumbs
⅓ cup brown sugar
½ teaspoon cinnamon
⅓ cup butter or margarine,
   melted

Filling:
1 quart Baskin Robbins Lemon
   Custard ice cream

1 quart Baskin Robbins French
   Vanilla ice cream

Cream Topping:
½ cup whipping cream
2 tablespoons sugar
½ teaspoon lemon juice
¼ cups walnuts, chopped

Blend together graham cracker crumbs with brown sugar, cinnamon, and butter. With the back of a spoon, press half of the mix to the bottom of a 9" springform pan. Chill the shell for one hour. Spoon Lemon Custard ice cream into crumb crust and spread into an even layer. Spread remaining crumb mixture on top of ice cream; freeze for 1 hour. Spoon French Vanilla ice cream on top of frozen crumb crust into an even layer.

Topping: To complete pie, make cream topping. Whip cream with sugar and lemon juice until peaks form. Spread attractively on top of torte. Sprinkle nuts on top to garnish. Freeze.

"Rather than using graham cracker crumbs between the two layers of ice cream, spread on a thin layer of your favorite chocolate type ice cream."

Baskin Robbins   **Glendale, California**

BOMBA LUIE

Serves 8 to 10

½ gallon good quality vanilla
   ice cream
3 cups macaroon cookies,
   crushed

½ gallon mint chocolate chip
   ice cream
1 small can chocolate syrup
springform pan

Soften vanilla ice cream at room temperature until it can be easily handled. Spoon half the vanilla ice cream into springform pan. Smooth and pack layer. Add 1½ cups macaroons to top of layer. Repeat one more layer of vanilla ice cream and top with the remaining macaroons. Spread layer of mint chocolate chip ice cream on top of macaroons. Press down firmly and freeze 24 hours. Remove from freezer about ½ hour before serving. Remove from springform pan to serving plate. Drizzle with chocolate syrup over top. Cut into serving pieces.

"Easy and elegant. A birthday request that's extra special!"

Linda Paskins   **Cordova Sr. High School, Rancho Cordova**

CHOCOLATE SUNDAE DESSERT

Serves 9 to 12

2 cups graham cracker crumbs
¼ lb butter, melted
¼ cup sugar
1 cup evaporated milk
6 oz. chocolate chips

10 oz. miniature marshmallows
½ gallon vanilla ice cream
(brick type)
chopped walnuts (optional)

Mix first 3 ingredients together and press ⅔ of the mixture into bottom of a 9 x 13" pan. Place in freezer and reserve remaining mixture. Place milk, chocolate chips, and marshmallows in top of double boiler. Place over simmering water and stir until melted and well blended. Layer slices of ice cream onto crumb mixture with chocolate sauce, making two layers of each. Sprinkle top with reserved crumbs. Freeze for several hours. (Chopped walnuts are a nice addition to the topping.) Cut into squares to serve. Store in freezer.

Lynette Englert　　　　　　　　　　　**Nova High School, Redding**

CHERRIES JUBILEE ON ICE CREAM

Serves 8

Crust:
1½ cups graham cracker crumbs
⅓ cup butter, melted
Baskin Robbins Vanilla ice cream
Baskin Robbins Chocolate Fudge
ice cream
whipping cream, whipped for
topping

Cherries Jubilee:
1 can (1 lb. 14 oz.) pitted Bing
cherries
¾ cup currant jelly
3 tablespoons brandy or cognac

Preheat oven to 375 degrees. Crush graham crackers in a blender. Place crumbs in a bowl and toss with butter until well mixed. With the back of a spoon, press the mixture to the bottom and sides of an 8" square pan. Bake 8 minutes; remove to a wire rack and cool completely. Freeze at least 1 hour. Spread a thin layer of vanilla ice cream over graham cracker crust. Then spread on the chocolate fudge ice cream. Freeze until ready to serve. Cut into squares and dollop with whipped cream and spoon on a generous portion of cherry sauce.
Cherries Jubilee: Drain cherries and heat just to boiling in a saucepan with jelly stirring constantly. In another saucepan, heat brandy or cognac over low heat. Pour over cherry mixture, ignite.

Baskin Robbins　　　　　　　　　　　**Glendale, California**

FROZEN LEMON DESSERT

Serves 16 to 20

1¼ cups graham cracker crumbs
1 tablespoon sugar
3 tablespoons margarine, melted

½ gallon vanilla ice cream
1 can (6 oz.) lemonade,
*   undiluted*

Combine first 3 ingredients and pat into 9 x 13" pan (reserve small amount of crumbs for top). Combine ice cream and lemonade with mixer. Put mixture into cracker lined pan and sprinkle with remaining crumbs. Freeze.

"You may substitute ice milk to make this dessert a little more fat free. Great for a crowd."

Donna Swennes   **El Capitan High School, Lakeside**

OREO DELIGHT

Serves 16

Oreo cookies
½ gallon vanilla ice cream

1 jar Mrs. Rich caramel topping
1 large container Cool Whip

Break up Oreo cookies into bite size pieces and layer into a 9 x 13" pan (reserve a few for topping). Spread the ice cream over the cookie layer. Evenly pour the caramel topping over the ice cream. Cover with Cool Whip. Break the rest of cookies over the top of the mixture.

"Very rich, so it will go a long way."

Antionette DeNeve   **Charles D. Jones Jr. High School, Baldwin Park**

TRIFLE OF MACAROONS AND LADYFINGERS

Serves 8 to 10

8 ladyfingers
⅓ cup strawberry jam
⅓ cup orange juice (make it
*   ½ cup if wine or rum is not*
*   used)*
3 tablespoons wine or rum
*   (optional)*
8 crushed macaroons
1 quart Baskin Robbins
*   ice cream*
½ cup whipping cream

3 tablespoons confectioners'
*   sugar*
½ teaspoon vanilla
¼ cup almonds, slivered
Sublime Strawberry Sauce*:*
(Makes about 2½ cups)
2 packages (10 oz. each) frozen
*   strawberries, thawed*
¼ cup strawberries jam
½ cup sugar
2 tablespoons cornstarch

Use a 1½ quart glass souffle dish. Split the ladyfingers in half lengthwise and spread with jam. Arrange them in a single layer, jam side up, around the dish. Combine the orange juice and wine and pour it evenly over the ladyfingers. Add the crushed macaroons in an even layer. Spread with slightly softened ice cream. Freeze for at least 3 hours. Before serving, whip the cream, vanilla, and confectioners' sugar together. Pour a layer of the strawberry sauce over the ice cream, then a layer of the whipped topping. Repeat sauce and whipped cream layers two more times. Garnish top with strawberries, if desired, and slivered almonds.

Sublime Strawberry Sauce: Pour syrup from thawed berries into a 2-cup measure. Add enough water to the syrup to make 2 cups of liquid. Mix the sugar and cornstarch and blend in the syrup mixture, stirring over low heat until it all comes to a boil and thickens. Stir in the strawberries and the jam.

Baskin Robbins   **Glendale, California**

CHOCOLATE ECLAIR

Serves 9 to 12

1 box graham crackers
2 small boxes instant French
  vanilla pudding
3 cups milk
1 tub (9 oz.) frozen whipped
  topping
3 oz. unsweetened chocolate,
  melted

3 tablespoons butter
3 tablespoons milk
1 teaspoon vanilla
2 tablespoons corn syrup
1½ cup powdered sugar

Line the bottom of a 9 x 13" glass dish with crackers. Beat pudding with milk till smooth; fold in whipped topping. Spread half the pudding mixture over crackers; repeat. Spread second pudding layer with final layer of crackers.

Frosting: Mix together the chocolate, butter, 3 tablespoons milk, vanilla, corn syrup, and powdered sugar. Chill 24 hours in the refrigerator before serving.

"This always makes a big hit at any occasion. Kids and adults seem to really enjoy this recipe. Enjoy!"

Linda Brayton   **Grace Davis High School, Modesto**

PINEAPPLE REFRIGERATOR DESSERT

Serves 8 to 10

6 oz. vanilla wafers
½ cup butter or margarine
1 cup confectioners' sugar
2 eggs, well beaten

4 large slices canned pineapple,
  cut up
½ pint heavy cream, whipped

Crush wafers and line buttered 11 x 7" cake pan with ¾ of the crumbs. Cream butter and sugar together until light and fluffy; add eggs and blend thoroughly. Spread over crumbs. Arrange pineapple pieces over egg mixture. Whip cream and spread over pineapple. Sprinkle remaining crumbs over cream. Cover with waxed paper. Refrigerate for 24 hours (may be frozen).

"From a friend, Barbara Kyles, in North Carolina. Great because you can make it ahead of time."

Linda Winzenread   **Whittier High School, Whittier**

RASPBERRY DELIGHT

Serves 8

¾ cup graham cracker crumbs
3 tablespoons margarine, melted
2 tablespoons plus 1 cup sugar
3 eggs, separated

1 package (8 oz.) cream cheese
1 cup heavy cream, whipped
1 package (10 oz.) frozen
raspberries

Combine graham cracker crumbs, margarine, and 2 tablespoons sugar. Press into 11 x 7 x 1½" baking pan. Bake at 375 degrees for 8 minutes. Cool completely. Beat egg whites until stiff; set aside. Beat egg yolks until thick. Add cream cheese and 1 cup sugar; beat until smooth. Fold beaten egg whites and whipped cream into yolk mixture. Pour into cool crust. Puree raspberries in blender and then swirl through mixture. Freeze.

Margaret Currier   **Nevada Union High School, Grass Valley**

CHOCOLATE MINT TRIANGLES

Makes about 24 triangles

½ cup butter or margarine,
softened
1 cup sugar
4 eggs
1½ cups (16 oz. can) chocolate
flavored syrup
1 cup all-purpose flour
Mint Layer:
2 cups confectioners' sugar

½ cup butter or margarine,
softened
2 tablespoons green creme de
*menthe ***
Chocolate Glaze:
6 tablespoons butter or
margarine
1 cup semisweet chocolate chips

Heat oven to 350 degrees. Grease 13 x 9" pan. In large mixer bowl, combine butter and sugar until blended. Add eggs; beat until smooth. Add syrup and flour; beat until blended. Pour into prepared pan; bake 25 to 30 minutes or until top springs back when touched lightly. Cool completely in pan. Spread Mint Layer on cake; cover and chill. Pour Chocolate Glaze over dessert. Cover; chill at least 1 hour before serving. Cut into about twelve 3" squares; cut each square diagonally into half.

Mint Layer: In small mixer bowl, combine all ingredients and beat until smooth.
* 1 tablespoon water, ½ to ¾ teaspoon mint extract, and 3 drops green food color may be substituted for creme de menthe
Chocolate Glaze: In small saucepan over low heat, melt butter or margarine; remove from heat. Add chips; stir until chips are melted. Cool slightly.

Hershey Foods Corporation   **Hershey, Pennsylvania**

STRAWBERRY SQUARES

Serves 12

1 cup flour, sifted
½ cup brown sugar
½ cup nuts, chopped
½ cup butter, melted
2 egg whites

1 cup sugar
2 cups fresh strawberries,
* sliced **
2 tablespoons lemon juice
1 cup whipping cream

Mix first 4 ingredients and bake in a shallow pan at 350 degrees for 20 minutes, stirring occasionally (these are the crumbs). Sprinkle ⅔ of the crumbs in a 13 x 9 x 2" pan. Combine egg whites, sugar, berries, and lemon juice. Beat at high speed for 10 minutes. Whip the cream and fold it into the mixture. Spoon this mixture over the crumbs. Top with remaining crumbs. Freeze 6 hours.
* Frozen berries can be substituted for fresh: use 10 oz. frozen berries that have been thawed, and reduce sugar to ⅔ cup.

"This is one of my favorite desserts ... no one can get enough of it."

Debbie Grove   **Piner High School, Santa Rosa**

FROZEN LEMON CRUNCH

Serves 6 to 8

1 cup evaporated milk, undiluted
juice of 1 lemon (about ⅓ cup)
2 eggs
½ cup sugar
½ teaspoon salt
1 tablespoon lemon rind, grated

½ cup graham crackers, finely
* crushed*
2 tablespoons butter or
* margarine, melted*
3 tablespoons sugar

Chill evaporated milk in an 8" square pan in freezer until soft ice crystals form on edges of pan (15 to 20 minutes). Pour into mixing bowl and whip until thickened. Add lemon juice and whip until very stiff (about 2 minutes longer). In a separate bowl, beat eggs, ½ cup sugar, and salt until thick and creamy. Fold in whipped milk and lemon rind. Spoon back into 8" square pan.
Crumb topping: Combine graham crackers, butter, and 3 tablespoons sugar and sprinkle over filling. Freeze about 2 hours until firm. Serve ice cold.

"Wonderfully light and refreshing. There is always room for this dessert, even after the biggest meal."

Judy Stinton   **Mt. Miguel High School, Spring Valley**

GRANDMA'S SUMMER TREAT

Serves 6

1 package Cool-Aid flavor of your
  choice

1 cup sugar
1 cup Pet milk

Mix all ingredients together in a bowl till sugar is dissolved. Pour into 9" square glass dish. Freeze for 3 to 4 hours until firm. Scoop and serve.

"Simple and easy. Kids enjoy it."

Janet Worland   **Silver Valley High School, Yermo**

SANGRIA SLUSH

Makes 10 one-half cup servings

1 can (8 oz.) crushed pineapple
2½ cups dry red wine
1½ cups orange juice

½ cup sugar
2 tablespoons lemon peel, grated

In covered blender container, blend first 5 ingredients for 5 seconds at high speed. Pour mixture into a 9" square baking pan. Freeze.
To serve, let stand a few minutes at room temperature to soften slightly. With a spoon stir until semi-thawed. Spoon into wine or sherbet glasses. Garnish with lemon peel.

"Great after a heavy meal."

Maridel Anagnos   **Tokay High School, Lodi**

FRENCH VANILLA ICE CREAM

Serves 6

½ cup sugar
¼ teaspoon salt
1 cup milk (whole or lowfat)

3 beaten egg yolks
1 tablespoon vanilla
1 cup whipping cream

Blend first 4 ingredients in saucepan. Cook over medium heat, stirring constantly just until mixture comes to a boil. Cool. Add vanilla and whipping cream. Freeze. For a summer favorite, add 1½ cup mashed fruit with ½ cup sugar to mixture before freezing.

"This has been a family favorite for 30 years. Strawberry for the 4th of July and peach for Labor Day!"

Jeri Lundy   **Grossmont High School, La Mesa**

Fruits and Gelatins

POACHED PEARS IN WINE

Serves 4

2 cups sweet white wine
½ cup water (approx.)
1 cup sugar
1 cinnamon stick
lemon peel
2 whole cloves
4 Bosc pears
ice and ice water
2 lemons
mint leaves
Pastry Cream:
3 egg yolks

⅓ cup sugar
1 cup half and half, scalded
¼ teaspoon salt
1½ tablespoons cornstarch
1 tablespoon flour
2 tablespoons hazelnut liqueur
½ teaspoon almond extract
½ cup heavy cream
Raspberry Sauce:
¼ pint fresh raspberries
2 tablespoons pear juice

Boil the wine, water, sugar, cinnamon, lemon peel, and cloves. Wash and peel the pears, leaving the stem intact. Slice the bottom of the pears evenly so that they stand upright. Remove cores from the bottom of the pears with the melon ball scooper and place in acidulated water. Add the pears to the wine sauce and poach until they are easily pierced with toothpicks (about 8 to 12 minutes for small pears). Drain pears, (keep wine sauce for other uses), wrap in plastic wrap, and place in ice water or refrigerator. **To make pastry cream**, beat together eggs and sugar until ribbons form in a medium sized bowl. Gradually whisk in half and half, then gently add salt, cornstarch, and flour. Cook mixture over low flame for 3 to 5 minutes, or until thick. Whisk constantly to prevent lumps or curdling of mixture. When thick, take mixture off of heat and add hazelnut liqueur and almond extract. Pour mixture into bowls and chill. When cool, add mixture to whipped heavy cream. Reserve four raspberries to place inside the pears. **To make raspberry sauce**, combine raspberries and pear juice in a blender and puree. Check thickness; it should be able to thinly coat back of spoon. If too thick, add 1 to 2 tablespoons water. Strain through cheesecloth. Pour into bowl and refrigerate.

Set up: Remove pears from ice water or refrigerator and unwrap. If pears are wet, pat dry with clean cloth. Stand pears upright and make a small cut near stem with the top of a knife. Insert a mint leaf into slit. Fill hollowed out core section with pastry cream. Place on plate sauced with raspberry sauce. Make design of choice with pastry cream forced through the end of plastic bags.

"This is the Gold Medal Winner at the Young Chefs of South Bay Contest at which many high school students competed. Our North High students won 3 gold medals and $500 scholarships each with this outstanding dessert to finish their menu."

Jane H. McGinty   **North High School, Torrance**

CHOCOLATE ALMOND TERRINE WITH RASPBERRY SAUCE

Serves 6 to 8

1 envelope unflavored gelatin
¾ cup cold water
4 eggs, separated
¾ cup sugar
1 cup semisweet chocolate chips
2 tablespoons milk
¾ cup chilled whipping cream
2 tablespoons amaretto liqueur
  or ½ teaspoon almond extract

Raspberry Sauce (recipe follows)
Raspberries or other fresh fruit
(optional)
Sauce:
(Makes 1 cup)
¼ cup sugar
2 teaspoons cornstarch
1 package (10 oz.) frozen
  raspberries, thawed

In medium saucepan, sprinkle gelatin over water; let stand several minutes to soften. In small mixing bowl, slightly beat egg yolks; add to saucepan. Stir in sugar; cook over medium heat, stirring constantly, until gelatin is dissolved and mixture comes to a gentle boil. Cook and stir 2 minutes more; remove from heat. Pour into bowl; cover with plastic wrap and cool, stirring occasionally, to room temperature. In small microwave-safe bowl, combine chocolate chips and milk; microwave at 100% high for 1 minute. Stir to completely melt chips; set aside.

In large mixer bowl, beat egg whites until stiff peaks form; gradually add gelatin mixture folding gently until combined. Beat whipping cream until soft peaks form; fold into gelatin mixture. Divide into 2 equal portions (about 2 cups each). Gently fold amaretto into one portion; pour into a 8 x 4" loaf pan, spreading evenly in pan. Cover; chill amaretto layer until partially set (about 20 minutes). Meanwhile, gently fold remaining gelatin mixture into chocolate mixture; keep covered at room temperature. Carefully spoon chocolate portion onto amaretto layer. Cover; chill several hours or until firm. Prepare Raspberry Sauce; cool. To serve, unmold dessert onto a serving tray; slice and serve with sauce. Garnish as desired.

Raspberry Sauce: In saucepan, combine sugar and cornstarch; stir in thawed frozen raspberries. Heat to boiling, stirring constantly; boil and stir 1 minute. Cool; press through sieve to remove seeds.

Hershey Foods Corporation   **Hershey, Pennsylvania**

RASPBERRY FONDUE

Serves 25

2 packages (1 lb. each) frozen
  raspberries, thawed
¼ cup sugar
¼ cup cornstarch

¼ cup cherry brandy or 1 ounce
  cherry flavoring
1 tablespoon lemon juice

Puree thawed raspberries, using a blender or seive. Pour pureed raspberries into a cold electric skillet; blend in sugar and cornstarch. Set temperature control to 250 degrees and stir raspberry mixture continually until thickened and clear. Stir in cherry brandy and lemon juice. Lower temperature to warm position and serve.

"May substitute strawberries for raspberries. Delicious dunkables for this fondue: angel food cake cubes, sliced bananas (dipped in lemon juice), or whole fresh strawberries."

Millie Deeton   **Don Lugo High School, Chino**

ORANGE DELIGHT

Serves 4 to 6

*3 navel oranges, peeled and
    sectioned
1 tablespoon honey*

*1 to 2 teaspoons cinnamon
½ cup flaked coconut (optional)*

Put orange sections into medium-size bowl. Mix with honey and cinnamon. Add coconut if desired. Let flavors blend at room temperature for 10 to 30 minutes.

"A family style recipe from my years in the peace corps in Tunisia. It's delicious!"

Judy Gross   **Lone Pine High School, Lone Pine**

RHUBARB CRUNCH

Serves 12

*2 eggs
1 cup sugar
4 tablespoons flour
3 cups rhubarb, diced*

*½ cup brown sugar
¼ cup butter
⅔ cup oatmeal*

Beat the eggs. Add sugar and flour. Fold in the rhubarb. Pour into greased 9 x 11" pan. Mix together the brown sugar, butter, and oatmeal. Sprinkle on top. Bake at 350 degrees for 30 minutes, until lightly browned.

"We make this a lot during the summer when rhubarb is plentiful. Serve with ice cream for a cool summer dessert."

Olga Erickson West
            Santana High School and West Hills High School, Santee

RASPBERRY DELIGHT

Serves 8 to 10

*1 package (10 oz.) red
    raspberries
½ cup water
¼ cup sugar
1 tablespoon lemon juice
2 tablespoon cornstarch
¼ cup cold water*

*25 marshmallows
½ cup milk
1 cup heavy cream
¾ cup graham cracker crumbs
¼ cup butter, melted
1 cup nuts, chopped*

Heat raspberries with water, sugar, and lemon juice. Dissolve cornstarch in ¼ cup cold water. Stir in berries; cool until clear and thick. Melt marshmallows in milk using a double boiler; cool. Whip cream and fold in marshmallows. Mix cracker crumbs and butter. Place crumbs into a square 8" pan and press into place. Sprinkle a layer of chopped nuts over crust. Spread marshmallow mixture over crumbs and berry mixture on top. Refrigerate overnight until firm.

Judy Hevener   **Porterville High School, Porterville**

MORE THAN JUST JELLO

1 box (6 oz.) any flavor Jello   *1 can crushed pineapple*
2 cups boiling water   *1 cup mini marshmallows*
8 oz. cream cheese, softened

In a blender, combine Jello and boiling water. When frothy, add and blend in the cream cheese. Add and barely blend (or just stir) in the crushed pineapple. Pour into a square 9" pan or comparable size. Top with mini marshmallows. Chill until firm. Serve on a bed of lettuce.

"Vary the Jello with holidays or color schemes. You can also top with chopped nuts or even coconut before serving."

Julie Hampton   **Millikan High School, Long Beach**

LIME JELLO SALAD

Serves 12 to 16

2 cups boiling water   *1 large can evaporated milk*
1 large package lime Jello   *1 pint cottage cheese*
1 large can crushed pineapple   *1 cup nuts, chopped (optional)*
1 cup mayonnaise   *1 teaspoon horseradish*
                                          (optional)

Pour boiling water over Jello; stir and cool. Add remaining ingredients. Stir all together in a large mixing bowl. Pour into a 9 x 13" glass dish. Refrigerate until firm.

Sue Nall   **Temple City High School, Temple City**

LEMON LUNCHEON SALAD

Serves 12

1 package (6 oz.) lemon Jello   *1 small can mandarin oranges,*
1 carton (8 oz.) Cool Whip   *drained*
1 medium can crushed
  pineapple, drained

Make Jello according to directions. When half set, mix Cool Whip, oranges, and pineapple thoroughly with Jello. Pour into 9 x 13" dish. Refrigerate until set. Cut into squares. For a nice effect, place a thinly sliced piece of lemon on squares.

"This makes a wonderful salad for buffets or a light dessert for a heavy meal."

Sandy Robertson   **Whittier High School, Whittier**

STRAWBERRY BANANA SALAD

Serves 8

2 small packages strawberry Jello
2 cups boiling water
20 oz. frozen strawberries

1 can (13 oz.) crushed pineapple,
drained
2 large ripe bananas
1 cup walnuts, chopped

Dissolve gelatin in water. Add berries, stirring occasionally until thawed. Add pineapple, banana, and walnuts. Pour into Jello mold. Chill until firm.

"This is a nice, cold side dish in summer or an easy-to-prepare fruit dish in winter."

Sheryl Malone   **Poway High School, Poway**

FRUIT SALAD

Serves 4

1 can (15 oz.) pineapple, crushed
and drained
1 package orange Jello

1½ cups cottage cheese
1 small package Cool Whip

Drain fruit well. Add dry Jello mixture and cottage cheese. Fold in Cool Whip and serve.
Variation: Substitute whipped cream and mandarin oranges for Cool Whip and pineapple.

"This is a family favorite with spaghetti or lasagna."

Elma Jean Mornac   **Hillside Jr. High School, Simi Valley**

MRS. B'S DESSERT

Serves 10

½ cup butter
2 cups powdered sugar
2 eggs, beaten
½ teaspoon almond extract

½ teaspoon lemon extract
small flat can crushed pineapple,
drained
½ pint whipping cream
½ lb. vanilla wafers

Cream butter and sugar; add beaten eggs; add extracts. Whip the cream (do not add sugar). Crush the wafers and arrange as the bottom layer in 13 x 9" serving dish. Spread the butter mixture on top, then the pineapple layer, then the whipping cream layer. End with crumbs as top layer. Refrigerate for 24 hours.

"Rich, but delicious."

Gage Jones   **South Pasadena High School, South Pasadena**

QUICK PEACH CRUMBLE

Serves 10 to 12

½ cup margarine
1 package yellow cake mix
1⅓ cups flaked coconut

1 teaspoon cinnamon
1 can (29 oz.) sliced peaches,
   drained
vanilla ice cream

In a glass 12 x 7" baking dish, melt the margarine at high power in microwave for about 1 minute. Stir in dry cake mix, coconut, and cinnamon; mix well. Remove and set aside 1⅓ cups of the mixture; press remaining mixture into dish. Microwave uncovered at high for 5 minutes, rotating dish half a turn once. Top with peaches and crumble remaining coconut mixture over top. Cook uncovered at high for 12 minutes, rotating dish half a turn once. Serve warm topped with ice cream.

"This tastes like an old-fashioned home-style dessert, but made quick and easy in the microwave!"

Penny Niadna   **Golden West High School, Visalia**

FRESH PEACH COBBLER

Serves 6

4 cups fresh peaches, sliced
1 tablespoon cornstarch
½ cup sugar
¼ teaspoon cinnamon
1 teaspoon lemon juice

1 cup Biscuit mix
¼ cup milk
1 tablespoon sugar
1 tablespoon margarine, softened

Mix and cook the first 5 ingredients till mixture comes to a boil and begins to thicken. Mix together the next 4 ingredients and drop in spoonfuls on the peach mixture. Bake at 425 degrees for 15 to 20 minutes.

"Delicious with vanilla ice cream too! Great summer dessert!"

Jeanne Koerner   **Temecula Valley High School, Temecula**

BANANA SPLIT CAKE

Serves 15

½ cup butter, melted
½ cup powdered sugar
2 cups graham cracker crumbs
2 egg whites
½ cup soft butter

2 cups powdered sugar
1 can (20 oz.) crushed pineapple,
   drained
3 bananas, sliced lengthwise
1 large container Cool Whip
sliced almonds for topping

Using a 9 x 13" cake pan, mix and press the first 3 ingredients into the pan to for
a crust. Mix the next 3 ingredients in a bowl, then spread over the crust. Spread the
drained pineapple over the egg white layer. Place the sliced bananas on the pineapple, then spread Cool Whip over the bananas. Top with sliced almonds. Chill in
refrigerator for 2 hours.

"Cool and delicious for a summer occasion."

Pat Smith   **Kern Valley High School, Lake Isabella**

FUN 'N FRUITY FINGER FOOD

Makes 9 treats

4 envelopes Knox unflavored
  gelatin

4 cups fruit juice (either apple,
  cranberry, orange, etc.)

In a medium saucepan, sprinkle unflavored gelatin over 1 cup juice. Let stand one
minute. Stir over low heat until gelatin is dissolved, about 3 minutes. Stir in
remaining 3 cups juice. Pour into 9" square nonstick baking pan. Chill until firm,
about 3 hours. To serve, cut into 2" squares or press cookie cutter shapes into
pan. Remove carefully with thin, flexible metal spatula.

"Easy and good ... even high school students like the shapes."

Gage Jones   **South Pasadena High School, South Pasadena**

PRETZEL SALAD

Serves 9 to 12

12 oz. cream cheese
1¼ cup sugar
2⅔ cups pretzels, coarsely
  chopped
1½ cubes butter, melted
¾ of 9 oz. carton Cool Whip

1 package (6 oz.) strawberry
  gelatin
2 cups pineapple juice
1 package (10 oz.) frozen
  strawberries

Soften cheese and beat together with sugar and set aside. Mix crushed pretzels and
melted butter and press into a 9 x 13" pan. Bake at 350 degrees for 10 minutes.
Cool partially. Spread cream cheese mixture over pretzels. Spread Cool Whip over
cheese and chill. Dissolve gelatin in hot pineapple juice and allow to set partially.
Add thawed strawberries to gelatin and spoon over other mixture. Allow to set.

*"A favorite from my sister-in-law that is served as dessert at Thanksgiving
time."*

Yvonne M. Jones   **Ceres High School, Ceres**

...N FLUFF SQUARES

...s vanilla wafers, finely
...ushed
...p pecans, chopped
...ablespoons butter or
  margarine, melted
2 packages (3 oz. each) lemon
  gelatin

1¼ cups boiling water
½ cup whipping cream
1 package (3 oz.) instant lemon
  pudding mix
1 pint lemon sherbet, softened

Combine vanilla wafer crumbs, pecans, and butter. Reserve ½ cup crumb mixture. Press remaining mixture into 10 x 6" shallow baking dish; chill. Dissolve gelatin into boiling water; cool to lukewarm. Whip cream till soft peaks form; set aside. Add dry pudding mix to gelatin; mix well. Add sherbet; beat at low speed until thickened and nearly set. Fold in whipped cream. Turn into baking dish; sprinkle reserved crumb mixture on top. Chill at least 1 hour. Cut into squares to serve.

"Light dessert to top off a meal."

Alcyone Bass   **Lakewood High School, Lakewood**

TWIN ANGEL CAKE PIE

Makes 1 cake

1 -inch prepared Angel food cake
1 envelope gelatin
½ cup cold water
4 teaspoons lemon juice
2 packages frozen raspberries

⅛ teaspoon salt
2 egg whites
1½ cups whipping cream
1 banana, sliced
1 cup flaked coconut

Cut cake horizontally into two layers. Hollow out both layers leaving shells one inch thick. Fill in tube holes with bits of cake. Soften gelatin in cold water and heat until dissolved. Add gelatin and lemon juice to thawed fruit and refrigerate until partially thickened. Add salt to egg whites and beat until stiff. Whip 1 cup cream. Fold egg whites and whipped cream into fruit mixture. Fill cake shells and chill. Decorate with ½ cup whipped cream, bananas, and coconut.

"Very light and summery dessert."

Karen Tilson   **Poly High School, Riverside**

EASY CALIFORNIA TRIFLE

Serves 10 to 12

1 package (6 oz.) strawberry or
  raspberry Jello
1 can (17 oz.) fruit cocktail,
  drained
1 purchased/prepared pound
  cake
¼ cup orange juice

1 large package vanilla instant
  pudding
3 cups milk
1 large container Cool Whip
¼ cup slivered almonds
7 to 10 maraschino cherries,
  halved

Prepare Jello according to package directions. Add drained fruit cocktail to Jello. Set overnight. Slice pound cake horizontally, forming 2 layers and cut into ½" cubes. Arrange cubes side by side in a 9 x 13" glass pan, leaving very small gaps between cubes. Drizzle with orange juice and let stand 10 to 15 minutes. Prepare instant pudding according to package directions. Spread over cake layer. Spread Jello and fruit mixture over pudding layer. Spread whipped topping over all. Decorate with nuts and cherries. Chill 1 to 2 hours before serving to set.

"This is also very attractive in a deep, round crystal bowl. Very rich and filling!"

Janet Policy   **Ramona High School, Riverside**

DAIQUIRI MOUSSE

Serves 6

4 eggs, separated
1 cup sugar
1 tablespoon lemon peel, grated
1 teaspoon lime peel, grated
¼ cup lemon juice

¼ cup lime juice
1 envelope plain gelatin
⅓ cup rum
1 cup whipping cream
lemon and lime slices

Beat egg yolks until light. Gradually beat in ½ cup sugar. Beat in lemon and lime peels and juices. Cook, stirring over low heat or use double boiler. Cook until mixture thickens but does not boil. Mix gelatin with rum and let stand for 2 minutes. Stir into hot mixture until dissolved. Chill until mixture begins to thicken. Beat egg whites until foamy. Gradually add remaining ½ cup sugar and beat until stiff peaks form. Whip the cream until stiff. Fold cream and egg whites into gelatin mixture and turn into 6 stemmed glasses. Chill until firm. Garnish with lemon or lime slices.

Judy Hevener   **Porterville High School, Porterville**

CHOCOLATE CLOUD

Serves 8

1 envelope unflavored gelatin
1/3 cup sugar
1/4 cup unsweetened cocoa

2 eggs, separated
2 cups skim milk
1 1/2 teaspoons vanilla

In a medium saucepan, mix gelatin, sugar, and cocoa; blend in egg yolks beaten with 1 cup of the skim milk. Stir over low heat until gelatin dissolves, about 5 minutes. Add remaining 1 cup milk and vanilla; chill, stirring occasionally, until mixture mounds slightly when dropped from a spoon. In a large bowl, beat egg whites until soft peaks form; gradually add gelatin mixture and beat until mixture doubles in volume, about 5 minutes. Turn into 8 dessert dishes or one 4-cup bowl. Chill until set, about 4 hours.

"Kids and adults like this one."

Sydney Fox   **Orange Glen High School, Escondido**

LEMON BAVARIAN CREAM

Serves 10 to 12

2 envelopes unflavored gelatin
1/2 cup water
2 packages (8 oz. each) cream
  cheese, room temperature
1 cup sugar
3/4 cup fresh lemon juice
3 teaspoons lemon zest
1 1/2 cups half and half
2 cups heavy cream, whipped

fresh mint and lemon slices for
garnish
Sauce:
2 tablespoons confectioners'
  sugar
2 tablespoons Creme de Casis
1 cup strawberry puree
1 cup strawberries, sliced

Soften gelatin in water. Heat until gelatin is dissolved. Whip the cream cheese until fluffy and light. Add the sugar, lemon juice, and zest. Beat until smooth. Stir in half and half and the gelatin. Refrigerate until mixture thickens slightly (about 30 minutes). Fold whipped cream into thickened gelatin. Pour into 2 1/2 quart ring mold or bowl. Refrigerate until firm. Garnish with mint and/or lemon slices and serve with strawberry sauce.

Strawberry sauce: Stir sugar and Creme de Casis into pureed berries. Add sliced strawberries.

"Will keep for 3 to 4 days when refrigerated."

Jan Jurgemeyer   **Mission Viejo High School, Mission Viejo**

STRAWBERRY SOUFFLE

Serves 6 to 8

2 envelopes unflavored gelatin
1 cup cold water
1 cup sugar
1 quart strawberries, washed and
  hulled
1 tablespoon lemon juice

1 teaspoon vanilla
5 egg whites
1 cup whipping cream, whipped
  whipped cream and whole strawberries for garnish (optional)

Sprinkle gelatin evenly over cold water in saucepan. Place over low heat and stir gently until gelatin is dissolved. Remove from heat and add ⅔ cup sugar. Stir until dissolved. Mash or puree berries in food processor or blender. Add to gelatin with lemon juice and vanilla. Chill, stirring occasionally until mixture mounds slightly from spoons.

Remove from refrigerator. Beat egg whites to soft peaks. Gradually add remaining ⅓ cup sugar and continue to beat until stiff peaks are formed. Fold beaten whites into berry mixture; then fold in whipped cream. Fold wax paper into 3 to 4 deep strips long enough to overlap easily when wrapped around top of a 6 to 8 cup souffle mold. Tie or tape into place. Pour berry mixture into mold. Chill until firm for several hours or overnight. Before serving, carefully peel off paper collar. Garnish with additional whipped cream, whole strawberries and leaves, if desired.

Theresa M. Campbell   **J.F. Kennedy High School, La Palma**

Pies and Pastries

RAISIN PIE

Serves 8

1 cup sugar
6 tablespoons flour
1 teaspoon cinnamon
½ teaspoon cloves
¼ teaspoon allspice
¼ teaspoon nutmeg
¼ teaspoon ginger

¼ teaspoon salt
1½ cups raisins
3 cups water
¼ cups vinegar
1 tablespoon butter
prepared pastry for 9 or 10"
double crust pie

Mix all dry ingredients in saucepan. Add raisins and water. Cook until thick. Take off heat and add vinegar and butter. Pour mixture into prepared pie crust. Cover with top crust. Bake at 425 degrees for 10 minutes and then at 350 degrees for 35 minutes.

"This pie was my great grandmother's specialty. My grandfather has told us many stories about her raisin pies."

Karen Bennett   **Norco High School, Norco**

GRAPE PIE

Serves 8 to 10

2 cups seedless grapes
   (Thompsons, Flames, etc.)
3 cups apples, peeled and sliced
1 cup sugar
3 tablespoons quick-cooking
   tapioca

¼ teaspoon ground cardamon
¼ teaspoon cinnamon
¼ teaspoon salt
prepared pastry for double crust
pie
2 tablespoons butter

Combine grapes, apples, sugar, tapioca, spices, and salt. Turn into 9" pastry-lined pie pan. Dot with butter. Adjust top crust; flute edges and cut vents. Bake at 425 degrees for 50 to 60 minutes.

"Grapes blend their honey sweetness with tart, juicy summer apples. You may wish to add a bit of lemon juice if grapes are overly sweet."

Betsy Cosart   **Monache High School, Porterville**

BEST BANANA CREAM PIE

Makes 1 pie

1 cup milk
1 cup light cream (or Pet
   canned milk)
3 tablespoons flour
1 tablespoon cornstarch
½ cup sugar
¼ teaspoon salt
2 egg yolks, slightly beaten

1 teaspoon vanilla
2 bananas, thinly sliced
1 baked pie shell
Meringue:
2 egg whites
½ teaspoon vanilla
¼ teaspoon cream of tartar
4 tablespoons sugar

Scald milk and cream in top of double boiler. Combine flour, cornstarch, sugar, and salt; mix together thoroughly. Add to scalded milk and cook 15 minutes, stirring constantly. Mixture should be smooth and thick. Pour over slightly beaten egg yolks. Return to double boiler and cook one minute longer. Cool and stir in vanilla. Arrange sliced bananas in baked pie shell. Pour filling over top of bananas.

Meringue: Beat egg whites with vanilla and cream of tartar till soft peaks form. Gradually add sugar, beating till stiff and glossy peaks form and all sugar is dissolved. Spread meringue over filling, sealing to edge of pastry. Bake at 300 degrees for about 15 minutes, or until golden brown.

"During my childhood, there was nothing I looked forward to more for dessert than 'mom's banana cream pie'."

Gerry Henderson   **Temple City High School, Temple City**

SOUR CREAM RAISIN PIE

¾ cup sugar
1 cup sour cream
1 whole egg, plus 2 yolks
½ cup raisins
1 tablespoon cornstarch
dash cinnamon and nutmeg

1 prepared pie shell, baked
Meringue
3 egg whites
¼ teaspoon cream of tartar
6 tablespoons sugar
½ teaspoon flavoring, if desired

Boil first 6 ingredients and pour into baked pie shell.

Meringue: Beat egg whites with cream of tartar until frothy. Gradually beat in sugar, a little at a time. Continue beating until stiff and glossy. Pile meringue onto pie filling, being careful to seal the meringue onto edge of crust to prevent shrinking. Bake until delicately brown. Cool gradually away from drafts.

Renee Paulsin   **Hemet High School, Hemet**

KEY WEST LIME MERINGUE PIE

Makes one 9" pie

3½ oz. flaked coconut
2 cups (about 40) vanilla wafer
  crumbs
3 tablespoons butter, softened
2 tablespoons brown sugar
⅓ cup cornstarch
1 cup sugar
¼ teaspoon salt

1½ cups water
½ cup lime juice
1 tablespoon lime peel
4 eggs, separated
2 tablespoons butter
¼ teaspoon cream of tartar
green food coloring (optional)

Crust: Spread coconut in a 9" pie dish. Microwave on full power for 5 minutes or until lightly toasted, stirring every minute. Mix in wafer crumbs, butter, and brown sugar. Remove ¼ cup of the crumb mixture. Press remaining mixture firmly into bottom and up sides of the pie dish, making a small rim. Microwave on full power for 1 to 1½ minutes. Cool.

Filling: In a 2-quart bowl, combine cornstarch, ½ cup sugar, and salt. Stir in water, lime juice, and lime peel. Microwave on full power 4 to 5 minutes or until mixture boils, stirring after every minute. Beat egg yolks in a small bowl with a wire whisk or fork. Stir a small amount of hot lime mixture into beaten egg yolks. Slowly pour yolk mixture back into lime mixture, stirring rapidly to prevent lumping. Microwave on 70% power 3 to 4 minutes or until mixture is thickened, stirring every minute. Stir in butter until melted. Pour filling into cooled pie crust.

Meringue topping: In a small bowl, beat room temperature egg whites and cream of tartar on high speed until soft peaks form. Continue beating on high speed, slowly sprinkling in remaining ½ cup sugar. Beat until sugar is completely dissolved and egg whites stand in stiff, glossy peaks. Spread meringue over filling, sealing to crust at edges so meringue will not shrink. Sprinkle reserved ¼ cup of cookie crumbs over top. Microwave on 70% power 2 to 3 minutes or until meringue is set. Chill.

"To make a yummy lemon meringue pie, substitute lemon juice and lemon peel for lime."

Rhonda Rohde Nelson   **Warren High School, Downey**

PAVLOVA

Serves 12

6 egg whites
⅛ teaspoon salt
2 cups granulated sugar
1 teaspoon vinegar
½ teaspoon vanilla

Topping
3 cups whipping cream
1 teaspoon vanilla
fruit of your choice (fresh or frozen)

Preheat oven to 275 degrees. In a large bowl, with mixer at high speed, beat egg whites and salt until frothy. Add sugar, 2 tablespoons at a time, beating well after each addition. Add vinegar and vanilla, and beat 10 minutes longer. Cut a 12 to 14" circle from brown paper. Spread meringue on circle. Place on pizza pan or cookie sheet. Bake 1 hour or until firm. Cracks are normal. Cool on wire rack. Place with paper on serving plate.

Topping: Whip whipping cream till stiff. Add vanilla and beat. Spread over meringue.

About an hour before serving, decorate with fruit, such as, sliced kiwi, frozen raspberries, or banana slices.

"Serve with a fine coffee."

Gloria Francuch   **Carpinteria High School, Carpinteria**

FRUIT 'N CUSTARD MERINGUE SHELL

Serves 8 to 10

¼ cup sugar
¼ cup flour
dash salt
1½ cups low fat milk
½ cup egg substitute, thawed
1 teaspoon vanilla
meringue shell
mixed berries or other fruit
strawberry sauce

Meringue Shell
margarine
4 egg whites
½ teaspoon cream of tartar
1 cup sugar
Strawberry Sauce
1¼ cups strawberries
1 tablespoon orange-flavored liqueur

Combine sugar, flour, and salt in medium saucepan. Gradually stir in milk. Cook and stir over medium heat until thickened and bubbly. Reduce heat and cook and stir 2 minutes longer; remove from heat. Beat egg substitute slightly, then gradually stir small amount of hot mixture into egg substitute. Return egg mixture to saucepan and cook, stirring, 2 minutes. Remove from heat and stir in vanilla. Cool filling slightly, then pour into meringue shell. Top with berries or other fruit. Serve immediately, with strawberry sauce if desired.

Meringue Shell: Generously grease 9" pie plate with margarine. Beat egg whites and cream of tartar in small bowl with electric mixer until foamy. Beat in sugar, 1 tablespoon at a time, until stiff and glossy. Do not underbeat. Spoon into pie plate, pressing meringue against bottom and sides. Bake at 275 degrees for 45 minutes. Turn oven off and let meringue stand in oven with door closed 45 minutes. Remove from oven and completely cool away from any drafts.

Strawberry Sauce: Combine strawberries and liqueur in blender. Blend to puree.

"So pretty and very impressive."

Shirley Marshman   **West Middle School, Downey**

TOLL HOUSE PIE

Serves 8

2 eggs
½ cup flour
½ cup sugar
½ cup brown sugar, packed
1 cup butter, melted and cooled

1 package (6 oz.) semisweet chocolate morsels
1 cup walnuts, chopped
1 9" pie shell, unbaked
whipped cream or ice cream

Preheat oven to 325 degrees. In large bowl, beat eggs until foamy. Add flour, sugar, and brown sugar; beat until well blended. Blend in butter. Stir in chocolate morsels and walnuts. Pour into pie shell. Bake at 325 degrees for 1 hour. Remove from oven. Serve warm with whipped cream or ice cream on top.

"Recipe may be doubled ... bake two pies and freeze one for later."

Joanne Fial   **East Middle School, Downey**

ANGEL FOOD PIE

Serves 6 to 8

4½ tablespoons cornstarch
¾ cup sugar
1¾ cups boiling water
⅜ teaspoon salt
3 egg whites
1 teaspoon vanilla
1 small can crushed pineapple,
    drained

¾ cup pecan or walnuts,
    finely cut
1 baked pie shell
½ cup cream, whipped
    (or Cool Whip)

Boil cornstarch, sugar, and water. Cook until thick; add salt. Beat egg whites until stiff. Slowly pour boiled mixture into egg whites, beating constantly. Add vanilla and pineapple. Pour into baked pie crust. Cool. Cover with whipped cream and sprinkle nuts on top.

"Light and heavenly dessert. Gets tons of raves!"

Janet Griffith   **Norco High School, Norco**

BANANA SPLIT PIE

Serves 8

3 sticks butter
2 cups graham crackers, crushed
1 tablespoon sugar (optional)
2 cups powdered sugar
2 eggs

5 bananas, sliced
1 can (13 oz.) pineapple, crushed
1 large Cool Whip
1 cup walnuts, chopped
1 small jar Maraschino cherries

Crust: Melt 1 stick butter and add to crushed graham cracker crumbs. Add sugar if desired. Spread evenly into a 9" pie pan. Bake at 350 degrees for 10 minutes. Let cool.
Filling: Beat powdered sugar, eggs, and 2 sticks softened butter. Pour into crust. Layer bananas, pineapple, filling, more bananas, and pineapple. Top with large Cool whip and sprinkle with walnuts and cherries. Refrigerate until ready to serve.

"If you get unexpected company, this is a dessert that will be a big hit. Rich and delicious."

Elma Jean Mornac   **Hillside Jr. High School, Simi Valley**

FRESH PEACH-KIWI ALMOND TART

Serves 10 to 12

*1 ready-made refrigerated pie
  crust*
*1 package (8 oz.) cream cheese,
  softened*
⅓ cup sugar
2 eggs
2 tablespoons almond liqueur
⅓ teaspoon almond extract

*fresh peaches, sliced (frozen may
  be substituted)*
fresh kiwi, sliced
1 tablespoon hot water
1 tablespoon almond liqueur
*3 tablespoons peach or pineapple
  preserves*

Preheat oven to 450 degrees. Place prepared pie crust in a tart pan with removable bottom. Press dough up sides of pan. Prick bottom of crust with fork. Bake until lightly browned, about 8 to 10 minutes; cool. Meanwhile, combine cream cheese and sugar. Beat until fluffy. Add eggs, almond liqueur, and almond extract; beat well. Pour into cooled crust. Bake about 20 minutes or until a knife inserted in the center comes out clean. Cool and refrigerate.

Before serving, carefully remove sides of tart pan. Arrange fresh peaches around outer edge and kiwi in center. Heat water and almond liqueur until hot. Stir into preserves. Brush peaches and kiwi generously with mixture.

"This is a delicious finish for a summer dinner or a very pretty dessert when you have offered 'let me bring the dessert'."

Sharon Turner　　　　　　　　　　**El Dorado High School, Placentia**

CUSTARD PEAR PIE

Serves 8

1 9" unbaked pie crust
*5 to 6 ripe pears (or canned, well
  drained)*
½ cube butter

4 rounded tablespoons flour
3 eggs
1 cup sugar
1½ teaspoons vanilla

Slice pears into pie shell, and then slice butter on top of pears. Beat together flour, eggs, sugar, and vanilla. Pour mixture over the pears. Bake at 350 degrees for 1 hour.

"From a pear rancher's wife."

Darlene Lupul　　　　　　　　　　**Tokay High School, Lodi**

LEMON CHESS PIE

Serves 6 to 8

3 eggs
1 cup sugar
1 tablespoon cornmeal
1 teaspoon vanilla

1 tablespoon lemon juice
½ cup butter, melted
½ cup milk
1 purchased unbaked pie shell

Place all ingredients in a large bowl and beat with an electric mixer till well blended. Pour into unbaked pie shell. Bake at 350 degrees for 45 minutes or until pie is set in the center.

"Easy and very tasty!"

Marilyn Tam   **Orange Glen High School, Escondido**

BLACK BOTTOM LEMON PIE

Serves 8 to 10

baked 9" pie shell	*3 tablespoons water*
2 oz. semisweet chocolate	*1 teaspoon lemon peel*
4 eggs, separated	*1 cup sugar*
¼ cup lemon juice	

Melt chocolate over hot water or melt carefully in microwave. Spread evenly over bottom of cool pie shell.

In top of double boiler (or medium-sized saucepan), beat egg yolks until thick and lemon-colored. Add lemon juice and water; mix well; stir in lemon peel and ½ cup sugar. Cook over hot (not boiling) water (or very low heat in saucepan), stirring constantly until thick; remove from heat.

Beat egg whites until frothy. Add remaining ½ cup sugar gradually, beating constantly, until stiff, glossy peaks form. Fold half of this mixture into egg-yolk mixture. Pour over chocolate in pie shell. Spoon remaining egg white mixture into pastry tube and make a lattice design on top of filling. Bake at 325 degrees for 10 to 15 minutes, or until lightly browned. Cool on wire rack.

"Until you've tasted the chocolate-lemon combination, you've no idea how good it is. From the Farm Journal's Complete Pie Cookbook."

Betsy Cosart   **Monache High School, Porterville**

SOUTHERN PECAN PIE

Serves 5

1 cup pecans, chopped	*pinch of salt*
1 9" deep pie shell	*1 cup dark corn syrup*
1 stick butter, softened	*3 eggs, slightly beaten*
1 cup sugar	*1 teaspoon vanilla*

Sprinkle chopped nuts in pie shell. In a bowl, cream butter, sugar, and salt. Add corn syrup, beaten eggs, and vanilla. Blend well. Pour mixture over nuts. Bake at 375 degrees for 40 to 45 minutes.

"A southerner's delight!"

Lenora Dugas   **Hoover Jr. High School, Lakewood**

IMPOSSIBLE BROWNIE PIE

Serves 6 to 8

4 eggs
1 bar (14 oz.) sweet cooking
   chocolate, melted and cooled
¼ cup Bisquick baking mix

½ cup brown sugar, packed
½ cup butter, softened
¼ cup nuts, chopped

Heat oven to 350 degrees. Grease 9" pie plate. Beat all ingredients except nuts until smooth for 2 minutes in blender on high, stopping occasionally to stir. Pour into pie plate; sprinkle with nuts. Bake for 30 to 35 minutes or until knife inserted in center comes out clean. Cool 5 minutes and serve with ice cream, if desired.

"A favorite with my students in the foods classes."

Joyce Grohmann   **Bellflower High School, Bellflower**

BIG APPLE PIZZA

1 cup biscuit mix
¼ cup water
1 cup applesauce
⅓ cup sugar

½ teaspoon cinnamon
⅛ teaspoon nutmeg
6 tablespoons flour
¼ cup margarine

Measure biscuit mix into a bowl. Stir in water lightly with a fork. Knead 5 times on a lightly floured board. Tear off a 10" piece of aluminum foil. Roll dough on foil in a circle to about ¼" thickness. Turn up foil and the edge of the dough about ½". Pour the applesauce into crust and top with crumb topping.
Topping: Combine sugar, cinnamon, nutmeg, flour, and margarine with the pastry cutter till crumbly and spread on top of applesauce. Bake in a preheated 400 degrees oven 20 to 25 minutes, or until the crust begins to brown.

"This recipe has been asked for over 20 years in my home ec classes."

Gwen I. Hansen   **Bloomington High School, Bloomington**

CREAM PUFF RING

Serves 8 to 10

1 cup plus 1 tablespoon water
½ cup butter
¼ teaspoon salt
1 cup flour
4 eggs
1 egg yolk

¼ cup almonds, sliced and
   blanched
2 cups heavy cream, chilled
1 cup powdered sugar
2 teaspoons vanilla extract
¼ teaspoon almond extract
extra powdered sugar

Preheat oven to 400 degrees. In saucepan, combine the 1 cup water, butter, and salt. Bring to boil, then remove from heat. Beat in flour with spoon, all at once. Mixture will form a ball and leave sides of pan. Remove from heat. Add whole eggs, one at a time, and mix between each addition. On baking sheet lined with brown paper, draw an 8" circle. Form a ring with dough on the inside of the circle (pastry bag works well). Bake 50 minutes.

In a small bowl, with a fork, beat egg yolk with the remaining 1 tablespoon water. Remove ring from oven. Brush egg mixture lightly over top of ring. Sprinkle with almonds. Bake 5 minutes more and then cool on wire rack.

Meanwhile, in medium bowl, combine cream, 1 cup powdered sugar, and extracts. Refrigerate, covered, for 1 hour. Place in a larger bowl of ice water and beat at high speed until stiff. With a sharp knife, split ring in half crosswise. Place bottom on serving platter. Pipe filling through pastry bag onto cut bottom layer. Set top in place. Sprinkle with more powdered sugar.

"I've prepared this for my classes to demonstrate how eggs are used as a leavening agent. It takes a while, but is a French delight!"

Jan Oliver   **Irvine High School, Irvine**

STRAWBERRY CREAM CHEESE COFFEE CAKE

Serves 6 to 8

1 package (3 oz.) cream cheese
4 tablespoons butter or
  margarine
2 cups Bisquick mix
1/3 cup milk

1/3 cup strawberry jam
1/2 cup powdered sugar, sifted
1 to 2 tablespoons milk
1/4 teaspoon vanilla

Cut cream cheese and butter into biscuit mix until crumbly. Blend in the milk with a wooden spoon. Turn onto floured surface and knead 8 to 10 strokes. Roll dough into a 12 x 8" rectangle. Spread jam down the center of dough. Make 2½" cuts at 1" intervals on lengthwise side. Fold strips over filling and pinch end together. Transfer onto greased cookie sheet. Bake at 425 degrees for 12 to 15 minutes. While warm, drizzle with glaze topping.

Glaze: Mix together the ½ cup powdered sugar, 1 or 2 tablespoons milk (as need to make drizzle consistency), and vanilla.

Joanne Montoy   **Esperanza High School, Anaheim**

EASY DROP DANISH

Makes 12

1/4 cup margarine, room
  temperature
2 tablespoons sugar
2 cups Bisquick
2/3 cup milk

1/4 cup preserves, any flavor
2/3 cup powdered sugar
1 tablespoon warm water
1/4 teaspoon vanilla

Mix margarine, sugar, and Bisquick until crumbly. Stir in milk until dough forms; beat 15 strokes. Drop by rounded tablespoonfuls 2" apart onto lightly greased cookie sheet. Make a shallow well in center of each with back of spoon; fill with 1 teaspoon preserves. Bake at 400 degrees until golden, 10 to 15 minutes. While warm, drizzle with glaze.

Glaze: Beat powdered sugar, warm water and vanilla until smooth.

"Quick, easy, delicious."

Marianne Traw **Ball Jr. High School, Anaheim**

STRAWBERRY TURNOVER

Makes 6

1 pastry for 10" pie crust
¼ cup sugar
1½ tablespoons cornstarch
2 cups fresh strawberries, sliced

½ cup confectioners' sugar
1 tablespoon butter, softened
1 tablespoon light cream

Prepare pastry as directed and place pastry for pie crust on an ungreased baking sheet, so that one half of the circle is centered on the sheet. In saucepan, combine sugar, cornstarch, and strawberries. Cook over medium heat, stirring constantly, until mixture thickens. Cool. Spread filling over centered half of circle; fold pastry over filling. Seal edges; turn up ½" of edge and flute. Cut slits in top. Bake at 425 degrees for 35 minutes.

Glaze: Blend together confectioners' sugar, butter, and light cream. Spread glaze over turnover while warm. Cut into wedges and serve.

Jan Neufeld **Fullerton High School, Fullerton**

PECAN TARTS

Makes 36 small tarts

1 package (4 oz.) cream cheese
½ cup butter
1 cup flour, sifted
¾ cup brown sugar
1 teaspoon vanilla

1 egg
1 tablespoon butter
¼ teaspoon salt
⅔ cup pecans, chopped

Crust: Mix cream cheese, butter, and flour. Chill. Make 36 small balls and press into miniature cupcake pans.

Filling: Beat brown sugar, vanilla, egg, butter, and salt until smooth; add pecans. Fill pastry-lined tins. Bake at 350 degrees for 25 minutes. Cool before removing.

"Delicious!"

Debbie Marks **Tokay High School, Lodi**

New York Chocolate Egg Cream, Page 91
Cappucino Cooler, Page 91
Chocolate Mint Triangles, Page 99

Sunburst Chocolate Cake, Page 152
Chocolate-Banana Sherbet, Page 156
Chocolate Dessert Timbales, Page 157

AWESOME APPLE DUMPLINGS

Serves 6

2 cups sugar
2 cups water
½ teaspoon cinnamon
¼ teaspoon nutmeg
2 cups flour
2 teaspoons baking powder
1 teaspoon salt

¾ cup shortening
½ cup milk
6 large apples, cored and pared
sugar
nutmeg
cinnamon
butter

Mix first 4 ingredients together to make syrup. Sift together flour, baking powder, and salt; cut in shortening. Add milk, all at once, and mix. Roll to ¼" thick and cut in 6" squares. Arrange apples on squares. Sprinkle with sugar, nutmeg, and cinnamon. Dot with butter, fold corner over, and press together. Place in pan and pour syrup over. Bake at 350 degrees for 45 minutes or until golden brown. Baste while cooking every 10 minutes.

"Great warmed with a scoop of vanilla ice cream!"

Charlotte Skee   **San Clemente High School, San Clemente**

CHERRY CHEESE PIE

Serves 8

1 package (8 oz.) cream cheese
1 can (14 oz.) sweetened
  condensed milk (Eagle brand)
⅓ cup lemon juice

1 teaspoon vanilla
1 9" graham crust pie shell
1 can cherry pie filling

In a large mixing bowl, beat cheese until fluffy. Beat in sweetened condensed milk until smooth. Stir in lemon and vanilla. Pour into crust. Chill 3 hours or until set. Top with desired amount of pie filling before serving. Refrigerate leftovers.

"It's very rich, but it's very yummy. Try other toppings such as blueberry, strawberry, etc."

Virginia Panttaja   **Sanger High School, Sanger**

FRESH STRAWBERRY PIE

Serves 6 to 8

2 boxes fresh strawberries
1 small package strawberry Jello
½ cup sugar
1½ cups boiling water

1 baked quick crust pie shell
whipped cream or dessert
topping

Clean strawberries, drain, and cut in half. Dissolve Jello and sugar in boiling water; pour over strawberries. Refrigerate to chill, stirring frequently, until Jello is very thick and syrupy. Pour into baked quick crust pie shell. Refrigerate till set. Top with whipped cream or dessert topping.

"Special recipe passed on by a very special lady, Ev Scott."

Marilyn Tam   **Orange Glen High School, Escondido**

JAGGER PIE (AVOCADO PIE)

Crust
1½ cups graham cracker
   crumbs
¼ cup sugar
¼ cup margarine, melted

Preheat oven to 325 degrees (300 degrees if glass dish is used). Combine crumbs and sugar, then add melted margarine. Press graham crust mixture into 9" pie pan and bake for 10 minutes. Let cool before adding filling.

Filling
1 medium or large avocado
1 can sweetened condensed milk
½ cup lemon juice

Place all ingredients into a blender container and blend until slightly thick, but smooth. Pour into cooled crust. Put into refrigerator and prepare the topping.

Topping
1 small carton whipping cream
2 tablespoons sugar
1 teaspoon vanilla
⅓ package almonds, sliced

In a medium bowl, place the whipping cream, sugar, and vanilla. Beat with electric mixer on high speed. About half way through mixing process, test to see if it needs more sugar. It is the right thickness to spread on top of filling when it forms slight peaks as beater is lifted out of mixture. Spread topping over filling; then top with almonds. Refrigerate 3 to 4 hours before serving.

"Very rich."

Helen Lievre
La Canada High School, La Canada

FRUIT PIE

Serves 6 to 8

¼ cup margarine, softened
¼ cup sugar
1 egg yolk
1 cup flour
½ cup sugar
3 tablespoons cornstarch
1½ cups apple juice
¼ cup lemon juice
1 teaspoon lemon rind, grated
6 cups assorted fruit (apples,
   pears, berries, grapes,
   bananas, orange sections)

Crust: Stir together ¼ cup softened margarine, ¼ cup sugar, and egg yolk. With pastry blender, mix in 1 cup flour until crumbs form. Press firmly into bottom and sides of a 9" pie dish. Bake at 400 degrees for 10 minutes. Cool.

Filling: In saucepan, mix sugar and cornstarch. Gradually stir in apple juice until smooth. Stirring constantly, bring to a boil over medium heat and boil one minute. Remove from heat; stir in lemon juice and rind. Cool completely and then fold in fruit. Turn into baked pastry shell. Chill 4 hours or until set.

"This pie looks beautiful and is practically a guilt-free dessert because of all the fruit."

Pat Hufnagel
Esperanza High School, Anaheim

PEANUT BUTTER PIE

Serves 8

¼ cup peanut butter
¼ cup powdered sugar
1 package (3 oz.) cream cheese
2 tablespoons milk

1 teaspoon vanilla
1 carton (9 oz.) Cool Whip
1 prepared chocolate crumb
  crust

Mix peanut butter, powdered sugar, cream cheese, milk, and vanilla. Fold in Cool Whip. Spread into crumb crust and refrigerate for 1 to 2 hours.

Carmen Leonard   **Mission Viejo High School, Mission Viejo**

FRENCH CHOCOLATE PIE

Serves 8 to 10

¾ cup sugar
½ cup butter, softened
2 squares (1 oz. each) chocolate,
  melted
1 teaspoon vanilla

2 eggs
1 8" baked pastry shell
whipped cream and walnuts for
  garnish

In a small mixer bowl, combine sugar, butter, chocolate, and vanilla. Blend well. Add eggs, one at a time, beating at medium speed 3 to 5 minutes after each. Pour into baked pastry shell. Chill at least 2 hours. Serve with whipped cream and walnuts.

"This is a wonderful! Everyone always wants the recipe!"

Lou Obermeyer   **La Sierra High School, Riverside**

CHOCOLATE CHIP PIE

Serves 6 to 8

1 cup chocolate chips
3 tablespoons milk
5 tablespoons sugar
4 eggs, separated
1 teaspoon vanilla

1 pie shell, pastry or graham
  cracker
whipped cream
chocolate shavings

Melt chocolate chips with milk and 2 tablespoons sugar. Cool slightly. Add egg yolks, one at a time, and vanilla. Beat egg whites with 3 tablespoons sugar until stiff. Fold whites into chocolate mixture. Pour into prepared pie shell. Top with whipped cream. Garnish with chocolate shavings if desired. Refrigerate.

"Very rich, but easy to make. Works well with either type pie crust."

Nancy Brunson   **Arcata and McKinleyville High Schools, McKinleyville**

CHOCOLATE SILK PIE

Serves 6 to 8

1¼ cup vanilla wafers, crumbled
1½ tablespoons sugar
6 tablespoons butter, melted
1½ sticks butter, room
  temperature
1 cup plus 2 tablespoons super
  fine sugar

1½ squares unsweetened
  chocolate, melted
1½ teaspoon vanilla
3 eggs
½ pint whipping cream
almonds for garnish

Crust: Combine wafers, sugar, and butter and line the edge and bottom of a 9" pie plate. Bake 7 minutes at 350 degrees, then cool.

Filling: Beat butter until creamy. Add sugar, a little at a time. Continue beating, then add melted chocolate and vanilla. Add 2 eggs and beat 3 minutes. Add remaining egg and beat 3 more minutes. Pour mixture into cooled pie shell and refrigerate. Serve topped with whipped cream and almonds.

"Easy to make and light, yet delicious! Great way to impress friends."

Karen Tilson   **Poly High School, Riverside**

HEAVENLY CHOCOLATE PIE

Serves 6 to 8

25 gingersnaps, finely crushed
⅓ cup margarine, softened
1 cup chocolate chips
1 egg, beaten
2 eggs, separated

1 cup heavy cream
1 teaspoon vanilla
whipped cream for garnish
shaved chocolate for garnish

Crust: Combine gingersnap crumbs and margarine. Using back of spoon, press cookie mixture around sides and bottom of a 9" pie plate. Bake at 375 degrees for 7 to 8 minutes; cool.

Filling: Melt chocolate chips over low heat. Remove from heat; add beaten egg and egg yolks and beat well. Beat egg whites until stiff. Fold into chocolate mixture. Whip cream until stiff. Fold cream and vanilla into chocolate mixture. Pile into crumb shell; chill. Garnish with whipped cream and shaved chocolate, if desired.

"This is a chocolate lover's delight!"

Gloria Walker   **Casa Roble Fundamental High School, Orangevale**

GRASSHOPPER PIE

Serves 10

4 tablespoons butter
16 Hydrox cookies
⅔ cups milk
24 marshmallows

1 cup whipping cream, whipped
2 oz. creme de menthe
1 oz. creme de cocoa

Crust: Place cookies in a plastic bag and use rolling pin to crush. Melt butter and mix with cookie crumbs. Press into bottom and sides of 9" pie pan; refrigerate (save some cookie crumbs for top of pie).

Filling: Scald the milk; add marshmallows and mix until smooth. Let mixture cool in refrigerator. Then add whipped cream, creme de menthe, and creme de cocoa. Pour mixture into pie crust. Sprinkle cookie crumbs over top. Freeze overnight. Allow to thaw 10 to 20 minutes before serving.

"An excellent 'make ahead' dessert for the holidays. I like to garnish with maraschino cherries at Christmas time."

Katie Placido   **Warren High School, Downey**

MOCK GRASSHOPPER PIE

Serves 6 to 8

*24 crushed Oreos (I do this in the
    blender)*
¼ cup butter, melted
1 jar marshmallow cream

¼ cup milk
2 to 3 drops peppermint
3 to 4 drops green food coloring
½ pint whipping cream

Crust: Crush Oreos and mix with melted butter. Press half the mixture into the bottom of a 10" pie pan or a 11 x 7" oblong pan. (Save the other half for top.)

Filling: Beat together the marshmallow cream, milk, peppermint, and food coloring. Whip the cream. Fold the marshmallow mixture into the cream. Pour into shell. Top with remaining crumbs. Freeze.

Roberta Priestley   **Alhambra High School, Alhambra**

TIN ROOF PIE

Serves 6

*1¼ cup chocolate wafers, crushed
    into fine crumbs*
2 tablespoons sugar
¼ cup margarine, melted
*1 quart Tin Roof ice cream,
    good quality*

½ cup chocolate syrup
1 cup whipping cream
⅓ cup sugar
½ teaspoon vanilla
½ cup chocolate chips

Crust: Mix crumbs, sugar, and margarine. Press mixture firmly and evenly against bottom and sides of 9" pie pan. Bake at 350 degrees for 5 to 7 minutes; cool.

Filling: Place slices of Tin Roof ice cream evenly over bottom of the pie crust shell. Pour chocolate syrup over top of ice cream and spread evenly with a rubber scraper. Place pie in the freezer. Whip whipping cream until it thickens; slowly add sugar and vanilla. Beat until imprints of mixer can be seen. Place spoonfuls on the pie and gently spread the cream over the pie evenly. Store, covered, in the freezer until ready to serve.

Garnish (chocolate leaves): Melt chocolate chips in top of double boiler. Wash and dry Camellia leaves, then dip the back side of the leaf in the chocolate. Place them on a wax paper lined tray and refrigerate. When hardened, peel off and place a chocolate leaf on each individual pie serving.

"Fast, easy, and very yummy! You may like to change the wafers, ice cream, and chocolate syrup to pecan cookies (such as, Pralines and Cream ice cream, carmel topping, and pecans for garnish).

Betty Byrne   **Arroyo Grande High School, Arroyo Grande**

BLACK BOTTOM PIE

Serves 6 to 8

20 graham crackers	*2 tablespoons cornstarch*
¼ cup sugar	*1 cup chocolate chips*
⅓ cup butter	*¾ teaspoon vanilla*
1 tablespoon unflavored gelatin	*¾ teaspoon rum or vanilla*
¼ cup cold water	*flavoring*
2 cups milk	*whipped cream and shaved*
4 eggs, separated	*chocolate curls for garnish*
½ cup sugar	

Crust: Crush graham crackers; add ¼ cup sugar and ⅓ cup butter and press into a pie dish. Bake at 375 degrees for 8 minutes. Chill.

Filling: Sprinkle gelatin over cold water. Heat milk until film forms across the top. Beat yolks until bubbly. Slowly add milk into egg yolk mixture. Mix ¼ cup sugar and cornstarch together; stir into milk mixture. Place over boiling water and cook, stirring constantly, until mixture thickly coats a silver spoon. Measure ⅔ cup cooked custard into a bowl. Add chocolate pieces and vanilla, and beat until well blended. Pour into cooled pie shell; chill.

Stir softened gelatin into remaining custard. Continue stirring until gelatin is dissolved. Chill until mixture is slightly thicker than consistency of unbeaten egg whites. Beat egg whites until stiff enough to hold soft peaks. Add remaining sugar gradually, beating until egg whites form stiff peaks. Gently stir in the custard mixture and rum/vanilla flavoring. Spoon over chocolate layer. Chill until firm. Serve garnished with whipped cream and shaved chocolate curls.

"Best dessert recipe I have ever found! It's a lot of work, but well worth it!"

Roberta Priestley   **Alhambra High School, Alhambra**

FROZEN YOGURT PIE

Serves 6 to 8

1 prepared graham cracker pie crust
1/3 cup fudge topping

1 pint vanilla frozen yogurt, softened
2 tablespoons chocolate cookie crumbs

Line bottom of crust with a thin layer of topping. Fill with yogurt. Sprinkle with cookie crumbs; freeze.
(Combinations are as endless as the selections at your nearby yogurt shop. Try fudge topping, peanut butter yogurt, and crushed Heath bar. Or use fruit topping, New York Cheesecake yogurt, and sliced fruit as garnish.)

"Yogurt is definitely a 90's dessert! A special thanks to fellow home economist and friend, Debbie Bush, for sharing this recipe with me."

Sue Hope   **Lompoc High School, Lompoc**

YOGURT PIE

Serves 6

1 container Cool Whip
2 containers fruit-flavored yogurt, prestirred

1 prepared graham cracker crust
1/4 cup desired fruit, sliced

Mix Cool Whip and fruit-flavored yogurt together. Pour into crust. Slice strawberries, bananas, or fruit of your choice on top. Refrigerate 3 hours (do not freeze).

"I like to use strawberry-banana yogurt."

Barbara Kimball   **Poway High School, Poway**

NUT BUTTER PIE

Serves 12 to 15

12 ounces chocolate wafer crumbs
1/4 cup sugar
1/4 cup (1/2 stick) butter, melted
1/2 gallon vanilla ice cream, softened

2 cups creamy peanut butter
1 cup clover honey
1 cup toasted cashews, chopped
2 cups chocolate fudge sauce, heated
2 cups whipped cream

Preheat oven to 350 degrees. Lightly grease 9" springform pan. Blend chocolate crumbs, sugar, and melted butter in medium bowl. Press into bottom and up sides of prepared pan. Bake 5 minutes; cool. Mix ice cream, peanut butter, honey, and cashews in large bowl. Spoon into prepared crust. Freeze at least 2 days. Place pie in shallow pan of hot water 10 seconds. Remove pie from pan. Top each serving with fudge sauce and whipped cream.

"This sinful pie must be made and frozen at least two days ahead."

Lynn Robertson   **Durham High School, Durham**

BERRY SCRUMPTIOUS PIE

Serves 10 to 12

2 cups flour
1/4 cup brown sugar
1/2 cup butter or margarine
1/2 cup pecans, finely chopped
3 cups blackberries, mashed

1/2 cup sugar
2 egg whites
1/2 pint whipping cream, whipped
2 teaspoons lemon juice
berries for garnish

Crust: Cut first 4 ingredients together till crumbly. Put into pan and bake at 350 degrees until brown, stirring often. Save half of crumbs for topping. Press rest on bottom of springform pan.

Filling: Beat berries, sugar, and egg whites in mixer for 15 minutes or until stiff. Gently fold in whipped cream; then fold in lemon juice. Pour into springform pan on top of crumb mixture. Freeze 12 hours to set. Garnish with berries and reserved crumb topping.

"This is a great tasting and easy 'make ahead' dessert. I've used strawberries too. If your springform pan is small and you have remaining mixture, pour extra into custard cups and freeze. Thanks, Jude!"

Janis Christopher   **Mt. Whitney High School, Visalia**

LIME GELATIN PIE

Makes 2 pies

1 cup flour
1/4 cup sugar
1 cup butter
1 package pecans, chopped
2 envelopes unflavored gelatin
1/2 cup cold water
1 cup sugar
few grains salt
8 egg yolks

1 cup fresh lime juice
1 tablespoon lime rind
few drops green food coloring
8 egg whites
1/2 teaspoon vanilla
1 cup sugar
1 1/2 cups whipping cream,
   whipped
1 tablespoon powdered sugar

Crusts: Combine the 1 cup flour with 1/4 cup sugar. Cut in the 1 cup butter using a fork; add pecans. Divide and spread in two pans and bake at 375 degrees till browned, about 8 to 12 minutes; cool.

Filling: Mix gelatin, water, 1 cup sugar, and salt in saucepan. Beat together egg yolks and lime juice and stir into gelatin mixture. Cook until mixture comes to a boil. Remove from heat and add rind and coloring. Chill until consistency is that of unbeaten egg whites. Beat egg whites until soft peaks form. Gradually add 1 cup sugar, beating until stiff. Fold beaten egg whites, whipped cream, and powdered sugar into gelatin mix. Pour into pecan crusts. Chill overnight.

"Takes a while to make, but well worth the time. I make it once a year for my husband's birthday because he is so special to us!"

Brenda Burke   **Mt. Whitney High School, Visalia**

PINK VELVET COMPANY PIE

Serves 8

16 graham crackers
¼ cup butter, melted
1 can (12 oz.) evaporated milk
1 small package Jello, any flavor

½ cup sugar
½ cup boiling water
¼ cup lemon juice

Crush graham crackers. Reserve ¼ cup crumbs for the top of pie. Mix the remaining crumbs with the melted butter and line the bottom of a 9" square pan with the mixture. Put the can of milk into the freezer for one hour. Mix the Jello with the sugar and add the boiling water and the lemon juice. Pour the chilled milk into a bowl and beat until stiff. Pour the Jello mixture into the whipped milk, beating constantly. Continue beating until stiff peaks form. Pour into crust and top with remaining crumbs. Refrigerate 3 to 4 hours.

"We like it with best with strawberry Jello. Great for a hot summer day when you want a cool dessert and a cool kitchen."

Loretta Salau　　　　　　　　　**Foothill High School, Bakersfield**

CREAM CHEESE PIE

Serves 10 to 12

Crust
1½ cups graham crackers, finely
  crumbled
⅓ cup margarine, melted
Topping
1 cup sour cream
3½ tablespoons sugar
1 teaspoon vanilla

Filling
4 packages (3 oz. each) cream
  cheese, whipped
2 eggs, beaten
¾ cup sugar
2 teaspoons vanilla
½ teaspoon lemon juice

Crust: Thoroughly combine cracker crumbs and margarine. Pat firmly into 9" pie pan.
Filling: Combine filling ingredients and beat until light and frothy. Pour into graham cracker crust and bake in a preheated oven at 350 degrees for 15 to 20 minutes. Remove from oven and allow to cool for 5 minutes.
Topping: Blend topping ingredients and spread evenly over entire surface. Return to oven and bake 10 minutes longer. Cool to room temperature and then refrigerate at least 5 hours before serving.

"Very rich. Always 'sinfully' delicious!"

Alice OKeeffe　　　　　　　　　**Walnut High School, Walnut**

POLITICIAN'S PIE

Serves 12 to 15

1 cup flour
1 stick margarine
1 cup nuts, chopped
1 package (8 oz.) cream cheese
1 cup powdered sugar
1½ cups Cool Whip

1 small box instant vanilla
 pudding
1 small box instant chocolate
 pudding
3 cups milk
Cool Whip for topping
Hershey bar, grated

Crust: Crumble together first 3 ingredients. Press into 9 x 13" pan. Bake at 350 degrees for 15 minutes and cool.

Filling: Cream together cream cheese, powdered sugar, and Cool Whip. Spread on cooled crust. Mix together puddings and milk until semi-thick. Spread on top of cream cheese mixture. Top with Cool Whip and grated Hershey bar. Chill and serve.

"Great recipe to take to a party or dinner."

Debbie Marks   **Tokay High School, Lodi**

BERRY LUSCIOUS

Serves 8

1 package frozen raspberries
¼ cup sugar
¼ cup water
3 tablespoon cornstarch
1 cup butter or margarine

1½ cups flour
½ cup walnuts, chopped
½ cup powdered sugar
12 oz. cream cheese
chopped nuts for garnish

Filling: (Make the filling first and set aside to cool.) Blend in saucepan, stirring constantly, the first 4 ingredients. Bring to a boil and simmer for 3 minutes. Cool.

Crust: Mix together in bowl the butter, flour, and walnuts. Press into a 9 x 12" pan and bake at 350 degrees for 15 minutes. Mix together the powdered sugar and cream cheese until fluffy; spread onto crust. Pour cooled filling over cream cheese. Top with Cool Whip. Garnish with chopped nuts.

"Makes a luscious dessert."

Marjorie Brown   **Cabrillo High School, Lompoc**

ALMOND CRUST CHERRY CREAM PIE

Serves 6 to 8

½ cup almonds, finely chopped
1 9" prepared pie shell
1 can sweetened condensed milk
½ cup whipping cream, whipped
½ teaspoon almond extract
1 teaspoon vanilla

⅓ cup lemon juice
1 pound can sour cherries, pitted
¼ cup sugar
2 tablespoons cornstarch
2 to 3 drops red food coloring

Crust: Spread almonds to coat the bottom of a regular pie crust and press down. Bake shell according to package directions; cool and refrigerate.

Filling: Mix the sweetened condensed milk with the whipped cream, almond extract, vanilla, and lemon juice. Stir until it thickens. Pour into shell.

Cherry glaze: Drain the cherries and save the juice. Combine juice, sugar, cornstarch and 2 to 3 drops of red food coloring. Cook over low heat until thick and clear. Add cherries and spread over cream filling. Chill.

"I make the crust the day before and chill overnight. My mother made this delicious pie for the holidays. It is very elegant and festive and would be a wonderful addition to any special meal."

Marty Willis   **Poway High School, Poway**

Puddings and Custards

MOUSSE IN A MINUTE

Makes 6 small or 4 average size servings

*1 package (6 oz.) semisweet
  chocolate bits*
1 egg
*1 teaspoon vanilla, or 1 tables-
  poon orange or coffee liqueur*

*1 cup milk, scalded
whipped cream and chocolate
  sprinkles for garnish*

Combine all ingredients in a blender and blend at high speed for 2 minutes. Pour mousse mixture into individual wine glasses or dessert cups and chill for several hours or overnight. Top with whipped cream and sprinkles, if you wish.

Pam Ford   **Temecula Valley High School, Temecula**

EASY POTS DE CREME

Serves 6

*¾ cup milk
1 package (6 oz.) semisweet
  chocolate pieces
2 eggs*

*2 tablespoons strong coffee
1 tablespoon orange flavored
  liqueur*

In a small saucepan, heat milk until small beads form around edges, but do not boil. In blender container, combine chocolate pieces, eggs, coffee, and liqueur. Blend until smooth. Add hot milk; blend again. Pour into 6 pots de creme cups, custard cups, or stemmed glasses; chill. To serve, add a dollop of whipped cream and sprinkle with cocoa.

"This is lighter in calories than traditional pots de creme. It is also quick to prepare and elegant to serve."

Merlina Phillips   **McCloud High School, McCloud**

BLENDER BREAD PUDDING

Serves 8

*2 cups milk
5 slices day-old bread
½ cup sugar
3 eggs*

*2 teaspoons vanilla
½ teaspoon cinnamon
½ cup pineapple, drained
¼ cup cherries, chopped*

Put all ingredients, except pineapple and cherries, into blender and blend well. Mix in pineapple and cherries and pour into buttered 8 x 12" baking dish. Set into larger pan of water and bake at 350 degrees for 45 to 60 minutes until golden brown on top.

"This makes a layer of bread pudding and a layer of custard while baking."

Marjorie Brown   **Cabrillo High School, Lompoc**

PERSIMMON PUDDING

Serves 6 to 8

1 cup sugar
2 tablespoons butter
½ teaspoon salt
1 teaspoon cinnamon
2 teaspoons soda
1 cup flour

1 egg
½ cup milk
1 cup persimmon pulp
1 teaspoon vanilla
¼ cup raisins (optional)

Mix sugar and butter. Add all dry ingredients and mix well. Add egg, milk, persimmon pulp, vanilla, raisins. Beat well. Pour into well-greased covered casserole dish. Set in pan of hot water and place in oven. Bake at 350 degrees for about 1 hour. Serve with a custard sauce or vanilla ice cream.

"This recipe has been passed down for generations in my family. As a child, we had a persimmon tree in the backyard, so this was the favorite dessert in my family."

Joyce Grohmann   **Bellflower High School, Bellflower**

CUSTARD PUDDING

Serves 8

4 eggs
½ cup sugar
pinch of salt

4 cups milk
1 teaspoon vanilla

Beat the eggs well and add the sugar and salt. Scald milk and pour over egg mixture, stirring constantly. Add vanilla. Pour into baking dish set in a pan of hot water. Bake at 350 degrees for about 1 hour, until knife comes out clean.

"This may be baked in individual custard cups in microwave on 50% power for 9 to 12 minutes. Let stand 5 minutes before serving."

Karen McCord   **Lindsay High School, Lindsay**

CHOCOLATE MOUSSE

Serves 4

1 package instant chocolate
  pudding
1¾ cup milk
1 cup Cool Whip

4 tablespoons creme de cocoa
4 to 6 tablespoons Cool Whip for
  garnish
1 small Hershey bar for garnish

Prepare pudding as directed, but reduce milk to 1¾ cups. Fold in 1 cup Cool Whip and creme de cocoa. Pour into dessert dishes and garnish each with a dollop of Cool Whip and a few chocolate curls. Chill for 1 hour.

"This is a great dessert for impromptu dinner parties and is always a hit!"

Jan Oliver   **Irvine High School, Irvine**

POMPADOUR PUDDING

Serves 6

½ cup sugar
2 tablespoons flour
⅛ teaspoon salt
2 egg yolks, beaten
1 egg, beaten
2 cups milk, scalded
½ teaspoon vanilla

2 egg whites
½ cup confectioners' sugar
1 oz. unsweetened chocolate,
   melted
½ teaspoon vanilla
⅛ teaspoon salt

Combine sugar, flour, salt, egg yolks, and whole egg. Add small amount of milk and blend; stir into remaining milk. Cook in double boiler, stirring constantly. Cool; add ½ teaspoon vanilla. Pour into sherbet glasses; chill.

Chocolate fluff topping: Beat egg whites and add sugar; beat stiff. Slowly add unsweetened chocolate, ½ teaspoon vanilla extract, and salt. Put on top of the pudding and chill.

"This is a childhood favorite that my mom, Mary Willis, used to make for special occasions. It is rich tasting, and a complement to any meal."

Marty Willis   **Poway High School, Poway**

LEMON LUSH

2 cubes margarine (Imperial)
2 cups flour
½ teaspoon salt
½ to 1 cup walnuts, chopped
Cool Whip and nuts for topping

Filling and Pudding Layers
1½ packages (12 oz.) cream
cheese, softened
1 carton (8 oz.) Cool Whip
½ cup powdered sugar
1 large box Jello lemon pudding
   mix (cooked type)

In mixing bowl, mix margarine, flour, and salt until crumbly. Then add walnuts, mix and pat into a 9 x 13" pan. Bake at 400 degrees about 20 minutes, until golden brown.

Cream Cheese Filling: With mixer, cream the cheese, Cool Whip, and powdered sugar and set aside.

Lemon Pudding Layer: Cook pudding using package directions and set in refrigerator to cool. Put waxed paper over top of pudding to keep from getting a hard crust.

After crust and pudding have cooled, spread cream cheese filling, then lemon pudding, over crust. Top with Cool Whip and nuts.

"Now enjoy."

Anne Silveira   **Central Valley High School, Central Valley**

PUDDIN' HOUSE

Serves 12 to 16

1 cube butter, softened
1 cup flour
1 cup pecans, finely chopped
8 oz. Cool Whip
1 cup powdered sugar
1 package (8 oz.) cream cheese,
  softened

1 small package vanilla instant
  pudding mix
2 cups milk
1 small can crushed pineapple,
  drained
1 large Cool Whip
¼ cup pecans, finely chopped
  (for topping)

Crust: Combine first 3 ingredients for crust. Pat into bottom of 13 x 9" pan. Bake at 350 degrees for 15 to 18 minutes. **Bottom layer**: *Combine Cool Whip, powdered sugar, and cream cheese. Spread on top of crust.*
Middle layer: Mix vanilla pudding, milk, and drained pineapple. Spread over the bottom layer. Top with layer of Cool Whip, sprinkled with pecans. Refrigerate 2 to 3 hours.

"This is so easy and always a hit when I make it. You can substitute chocolate pudding without pineapples for the middle layer."

Lou Obermeyer   **La Sierra High School, Riverside**

FIVE-LAYER DELIGHT

Serves 12 to 15

1½ cups flour
¾ cup margarine, softened
½ cup pecans, chopped
1 package (8 oz.) cream cheese,
  softened
1 carton (9 oz.) Cool Whip
1 cup powdered sugar

2 small packages instant
  chocolate pudding
3 cups milk
2 small packages instant
  lemon pudding
3 cups milk
chopped nuts or toasted coconut

Layer 1: Combine flour, margarine, and pecans until well blended, using fingers. Press into 9 x 13" pan. Bake at 350 degrees for 25 to 30 minutes. Cool.
Layer 2: Mix cream cheese, half carton Cool Whip, and powdered sugar; spread over crust.
Layer 3: Blend chocolate pudding mix with 3 cups milk and spread over layer 2.
Layer 4: Blend lemon pudding mix with 3 cups milk and spread over layer 3.
Layer 5: Top with remaining Cool Whip and sprinkle with chopped nuts or toasted coconut. Chill.

"A favorite of my mother-in-law!"

Diana Lee   **Elsinore Jr. High School, Lake Elsinore**

CHOCOLATE TRIFLE

1 pound cake, sliced
½ to 1 cup Kahlua
1 large package instant
  chocolate pudding

2 to 3 bananas, sliced
1 large carton whipping cream,
  whipped
½ bag Hershey's mini chips

In a large glass bowl, put a layer of pound cake and sprinkle with Kahlua. Spread with layers of chocolate pudding, banana slices, whipped cream, and mini chips. Repeat layers 2 to 3 times. Can be made several hours in advance.

'This is a family favorite at our Christmas luncheon.''

Jan Hirth   **Saddleback High School, Santa Ana**

BANANA AND BRANDY PARFAIT

Serves 4

2 bananas, sliced
4 tablespoons brandy
4 jiggers Grand Mariner

12 ounces Baskin Robbins vanilla
  ice cream
1 small container whipped
  topping

Heavenly Hot Fudge Sauce:

Makes about 2 cups

½ cup sugar
⅓ cup light cream

2 packages (4 oz. each) sweet
  cooking chocolate, broken into
  chunks
2 squares (2 oz. each)
  unsweetened chocolate

Marinate bananas in brandy for several hours. Then put a half jigger of Grand Mariner into the bottom of each dessert glass. Start layering ice cream, whipped topping, more Grand Mariner, Hot Fudge Sauce, more whipped topping, and ending with brandied bananas.

Hot Fudge Sauce:

In a double boiler, mix together the sugar and about half the cream, stirring over boiling water until the sugar is melted. Turn off the heat, and leaving the top of the double boiler in place, add the chocolate and stir until melted. Then add the rest of the cream.

Baskin Robbins   **Glendale, California**

Quick Breads

BANANA NUT BREAD

Makes 1 regular loaf or 3 small loaves

⅓ cup shortening	¾ teaspoon salt
⅔ cup sugar	1 cup mashed bananas (2 or 3
2 eggs	bananas)
1¾ cups flour, sifted	½ cup chopped walnuts,
½ teaspoon baking powder	if desired
½ teaspoon baking soda	

Cream shortening and sugar together until fluffy. Add eggs and beat. Sift dry ingredients (flour, baking powder, baking soda, salt) together and add alternately with mashed bananas, beginning and ending with dry ingredients. Stir to combine well, but don't overbeat. Add walnuts, if desired. Pour into one large loaf or three small loaf pans and bake at 350 degrees for 40 to 45 minutes.

"My grandmother's recipe has taken first place in the county fair competition."

Adrienne Steele   **Lee Jr. High School, Woodland**

OLD FASHIONED CARROT CAKE

Makes one loaf

1⅓ cups sugar	1 teaspoon nutmeg
1⅓ cups cold water	1 teaspoon cloves
1 cup raisins	2 cups flour
2 tablespoons shortening	2 teaspoons baking soda
2 cups raw carrots, grated	1 teaspoon salt
1 teaspoon cinnamon	1 cup nuts, chopped (optional)

Boil first 8 ingredients together about 5 minutes to make a syrup; cool. Sift together the flour, baking soda, and salt and then stir in nuts if desired. Add to the syrup mixture. Pour into a bread pan that has been lined with wax paper (or greased and floured). Bake at 350 degrees for 1 hour, or until toothpick inserted in the center comes out clean.

"This recipe was given as a shower gift to my mother before her wedding in 1930. It was during the depression, and people were poor so the wedding shower guests were asked to bring a traditional family recipe. This is one of them, and we have had it at Christmas for as long as I can remember."

Barbara Warren   **Colton High School, Colton**

DATE NUT BREAD

Makes 3 to 5 small loaves

1 package dates, chopped	2 eggs
½ cup water	1 teaspoon vanilla
2 teaspoons soda	2 cups sugar
1 tablespoon shortening	3 cups flour
1 teaspoon salt	1 cup nuts, chopped

Place dates and water into saucepan and bring to a boil. Pour off water and save enough to make 1½ cups. Add soda to water; set aside. Cream together shortening, salt, eggs, vanilla, and sugar (do this while dates come to a boil). Add hot dates to flour alternately with hot soda water. Add chopped nuts. Pour into 3 to 5 small greased loaf pans and bake at 350 degrees for 40 minutes, or more, until done.

"A favorite Christmas bread."

Simone Clements   **Bret Harte High School, Altaville**

FABULOUS LEMON BREAD

Makes 1 standard or 3 mini loaves

½ cup butter	*½ teaspoon salt*
1 cup sugar	*½ cup milk*
2 eggs	*1 tablespoon lemon peel, grated*
½ teaspoon almond extract	*½ cup walnuts, chopped*
1½ cups flour, sifted	*¼ cup (or more) lemon juice*
1 teaspoon baking powder	*¼ cup granulated sugar*

Cream butter and sugar well; beat in eggs; add extract. Sift together dry ingredients and add to first mixture alternately with milk. Blend just to mix. Fold in peel and nuts. Bake at 350 degrees for 30 to 35 minute (standard loaf) or 45 minutes (mini loaves) in well-buttered loaf pan(s). While still in pan(s) and warm from oven, mix together the lemon juice and sugar and spoon mixture onto bread (poke holes with toothpick to make it soak in better). Cool 10 minutes and turn out of pan.

"Best when warm. Sure to get raves!!"

Phyllis Kaylor   **Ray Kroc Middle School, San Diego**

LUSCIOUS LEMON LOAF

Makes 4 to 8 loaves

2 packages yellow cake mix	*2 medium packages lemon Jello*
5 eggs	*2¼ cups powdered sugar, sifted*
1 cup oil	*juice and grated rind of 2 lemons*
2 cups water	

Grease and flour either 4 large loaf pans, **or** 6 to 8 small ones **or** two 9 x 13" pans. Combine first 5 ingredients and beat for 4 minutes. Pour into pans. Bake at preheated 350 degrees for 35 to 40 minutes. Remove from oven and prick holes all over top with toothpick. Pour lemon icing over top while loaves are still hot (remove loaves from pans first so icing can drizzle down sides).
Icing: Combine powdered sugar and lemon juice and rind. Stir until well blended and smooth.

"This is moist and tangy! Great for holiday gift-giving. Easy, quick, and makes lots of mini loaves."

Colleen Easton   **Brea Olinda High School, Brea**

PUMPKIN BREAD

Serves 10 to 12

1¾ cups sugar
1¾ cups flour
1 teaspoon baking powder
1 teaspoon baking soda
½ teaspoon salt
½ teaspoon cinnamon
½ teaspoon cloves

½ teaspoon nutmeg
¾ cup oil
2 eggs
1 cup pumpkin
1 cup nuts, chopped
½ cup raisins (optional)

Put all dry ingredients in bowl and mix well. Add oil, eggs, and pumpkin, and mix well. Mix in nuts and raisins and pour into 2 large 9 x 5" or 4 small 3 x 5" greased and floured pans. Bake at 325 degrees for 45 minutes. Turn out of pans at once. Let cool and wrap tightly in wrap. Freezes very well.

"Brandi and Misti Kimmell, two of my students, brought me a loaf of pumpkin bread that their mother baked. It was moist and not too 'pumpkinish' so I begged the girls for their mother's recipe. It has been a real hit during our Christmas labs."

Carole Jackson　　　　　　　　**Apple Valley High School, Apple Valley**

POPPY SEED CAKE

Makes 1 loaf

½ cup (2 oz.) poppy seeds
¾ cup milk
¾ cup (1½ sticks) butter,
　softened
3 eggs

1 cup sugar
1 teaspoon vanilla
2 teaspoons baking powder
2 cups flour, sifted

Combine poppy seeds and milk in a large bowl. Let stand at room temperature 3 to 4 hours. Let butter and eggs warm to room temperature for easy mixing. Butter should be very soft. Preheat oven to 350 degrees. Add the rest of the ingredients to the poppy seed mixture, and beat at medium speed with electric mixer for 1 minute. Pour into greased and floured loaf pan. Bake for 1 hour and 15 minutes. Cool in pan for 5 minutes, then loosen and turn out to cool.

"This great cake-like bread is a family hit served plain, with powdered sugar or whipped cream, or even toasted!"

Sheryl Malone　　　　　　　　**Poway High School, Poway**

BUTTERSCOTCH RING

1 loaf (1 lb.) Bridgford Frozen
　Bread Dough, **or**
1 package Bridgford Frozen Roll
　Dough
1 package (3¾ oz.) butterscotch
　pudding (not instant)

1 cup brown sugar
1 cup walnuts, sliced
½ cup butter or margarine,
　melted
1 teaspoon cinnamon

Thaw bread or roll dough until pliable. Grease a bundt pan. Sprinkle ½ cup brown sugar on bottom of pan, top with walnuts; set aside. In small bowl, combine pudding mix, remaining ½ cup brown sugar, and cinnamon. Cut thawed loaf into 24 pieces (rolls do not need to be cut). Dip each piece in melted butter, then roll in butterscotch mixture. Arrange dough balls on top of nut mixture in pan. The bundt pan should be filled at least half-way with dough. Let rise in warm place until almost doubled, about 1 hour. The dough should rise to just under the top of the pan. Bake at 350 degrees for 35 to 40 minutes. Turn out of pan immediately and serve warm.

Bridgford Foods   **Anaheim, California**

STRAWBERRY BREAD

Makes 2 loaves

4 eggs
1½ cups corn oil
2 cups frozen strawberries,
  thawed
2 cups sugar

3 cups flour
1 tablespoon cinnamon
1 teaspoon salt
1 teaspoon soda
1¼ cups walnuts, chopped

Beat eggs, oil, and strawberries in a large bowl. Mix in the sugar. Combine dry ingredients and blend into egg mixture until smooth. Stir in chopped nuts. Pour batter into two greased loaf pans. Bake at 350 degrees for 1 hour or until done.

"This bread is great at breakfast time. Heat it and spread slices with butter or cream cheese."

Susan Sullivan   **Caruthers High School, Caruthers**

STRAWBERRY BREAD AND SPREAD

Approximately 30 sandwiches

3 cups flour
1 teaspoon baking soda
1 teaspoon cinnamon
2 cups sugar
1 teaspoon salt
2 packages (10 oz. each) frozen
  strawberries, thawed

1¼ cups vegetable oil
4 eggs, well beaten
1 teaspoon red food coloring
½ cup strawberry juice
1 package (8 oz.) cream cheese,
  softened

Mix all dry ingredients together. Make a hole in the center of mixture. Reserve ½ cup strawberry juice from thawed strawberries for spread. Pour strawberries, oil, and eggs into the hole. Mix by hand until all ingredients are thoroughly combined. Add food coloring. Pour into 2 greased and floured 9 x 5" loaf pans. Bake at 350 degrees for 1 hour. Cool thoroughly. For spread, combine the ½ cup strawberry juice and cream cheese until spreading consistency. Spread on cooled bread and make sandwiches.

"This delicious bread made into tea sandwiches was served at one of the bridal showers given for my daughter. I had to have the recipe."

Judy Banks   **Temecula Valley High School, Temecula**

ZUCCHINI PINEAPPLE NUT BREAD

Makes 2 loaves

3 eggs, beaten
1 cup oil
2 cups sugar
2 teaspoons vanilla
2 cups zucchini, grated
1 cup pineapple, crushed and
    drained
3 cups flour

2 teaspoons baking soda
1 teaspoon salt
1½ teaspoons baking powder
1½ teaspoons cinnamon
¾ teaspoon nutmeg
1 cup pecans or walnuts, chopped
1 cup raisins

Mix eggs, oil, sugar, and vanilla together. Add the zucchini and pineapple. Combine the dry ingredients and add to the zucchini mixture, mixing well. Add nuts and raisins and blend. Pour into 2 greased and floured loaf pans. Bake at 350 degrees for 55 to 60 minutes. Cool for 10 minutes in the pan, then turn onto racks.

"Very moist; freezes well."

Sally Spieker Slaughter   **Tehachapi High School, Tehachapi**

CHERRY CHEESE RING-AROUND

Serves 10 to 12

1 loaf (1 lb.) Bridgford Frozen
    Bread Dough
1 cup cherry pie filling
4 ounces cream cheese, softened

¼ cup nuts, chopped
2 tablespoons sugar
1 teaspoon vanilla

Let frozen dough thaw to room temperature. Grease tube pan (a 9" pie pan with ovenproof custard cup inverted in center to form ring can be used instead). Spread cherry pie filling on bottom of pan. Sprinkle 3 tablespoons of chopped nuts on top of cherry pie filling. Cut loaf into 20 pieces. Mix sugar, cream cheese, vanilla, and remainder of nuts. Place spoonful of cream cheese mixture in middle of each piece of dough. Seal edges around cream cheese to form ball. Place balls in double row in pan on top of cherry pie filling and nuts. Let dough rise in warm place until it triples in size. Bake at 375 degrees for 30 to 35 minutes. Turn ring out onto serving plate by placing plate on top of tube pan and turning over. Spoon any remaining cherry topping onto ring. Serve hot from the oven or cooled.

Bridgford Foods   **Anaheim, California**

SOUR CREAM POUND CAKE

Serves 8 to 10

½ cup margarine or butter
1¼ cups sugar
3 eggs
⅛ teaspoon salt

1½ cups flour, sifted
¼ teaspoon baking soda
½ cup sour cream
1 teaspoon vanilla

Cream together the butter and sugar. Add eggs one at a time, and beat after each addition until smooth and well blended. Add salt to sifted flour. Add one third of the sifted flour/salt mixture at a time, mixing after each addition. Stir soda into the sour cream, then add to flour mixture. Stir in vanilla. Pour into greased 9 x 5 x 3" loaf pan, lined on the bottom with wax paper. Bake at 325 degrees for 55 to 60 minutes. Cool for 10 minutes before removing from the pan.

"This recipe may easily be doubled and baked in a tube pan. Baking time may be a little longer. Use toothpick to check for doneness."

Eleanor Magorien   **El Toro High School, El Toro**

AUNT CHARLOTTE'S TORTE

Makes one 9 x 5" loaf

4 eggs
2 cubes butter or margarine,
  softened
2½ cups (1 lb. box) brown sugar

2½ cups flour
1 pound orange slice candies,
  cut up
2½ cups walnuts, chopped

Beat eggs together. Mix together with other ingredients in the order listed. Bake in greased loaf pan in 250 degrees oven for 2½ hours. To serve, slice very thin after loaf has cooled.

"Tastes like candy and keeps for a couple of weeks if wrapped well."

Kay Linberger   **Tokay High School, Lodi**

JUMBO BANANA NUT MUFFINS

Makes approximately 1 dozen

1 cup all purpose flour
1 cup whole wheat flour
1 teaspoon baking powder
1 teaspoon baking soda
¼ teaspoon salt
½ cup margarine or butter

½ cup sugar
2 eggs
1⅓ cups bananas, mashed
¼ cup milk
1 teaspoon vanilla
1 cup nuts, broken

Combine all dry ingredients. Cut in the margarine. Beat eggs; add milk, vanilla, and sugar. Mix well. Combine egg mixture and dry ingredients. Add mashed bananas. Stir in nuts. Grease bottom of muffin tin or use cupcake paper lines. Fill muffin tins almost to the top. Bake at 375 degrees for 25 to 30 minutes. Cool 5 minutes and them remove from muffin pan.

"These muffins smell great as they bake."

Laurie Owen   **Hoover High School, San Diego**

CINNAMON STICKY BREAD

Makes one loaf

2 loaves frozen bread dough,
   thawed
½ cup margarine or butter,
   divided
¾ cup sugar
1 teaspoon ground cinnamon

¼ cup water
½ cup brown sugar, packed
¼ cup raisins
¼ cup walnuts or pecans,
   chopped

Break apart thawed dough and form into 2" balls. Set aside in a warm place. Melt butter and set aside. In a shallow bowl, mix sugar and cinnamon. Place ¼ cup of melted butter in a small microwave bowl; add water and brown sugar. Microwave at high for one minute, until ingredients blend. Pour mixture into a 12-cup Bundt pan. Sprinkle with nuts and raisins. Dip bread dough balls in remaining butter, then roll in cinnamon/sugar mixture. Place balls in pan, stacking one layer on another. Bake at 350 degrees for 50 minutes. Cool slightly, then invert on a serving plate.

"Caution: addictive!"

Nanci Burkhart   **Hueneme High School, Oxnard**

STICKY BUNS

Makes about 12

1 bag frozen Bridgeford rolls
1½ sticks margarine or butter,
   melted
1 cup brown sugar

1 small package butterscotch
   pudding (not instant)
1 cup walnuts or pecans, chopped
cinnamon to taste

Thoroughly grease a bundt cake pan. Place frozen rolls inside (you may need to break apart). Melt margarine or butter and add brown sugar. Sprinkle pudding mix over rolls. Combine melted butter and brown sugar and drizzle mixture over rolls. You may wish to use a knife to get in between rolls so mixture will be between all rolls. Sprinkle with chopped nuts and cinnamon. Cover with greased foil and leave overnight to rise. Bake at 350 degrees for 30 minutes. Cool slightly and invert onto platter so caramel mixture will drizzle downward. Pull apart sections.

"Great as a dessert or even breakfast or brunch item. Always a hit when taken to get togethers."

Karen Frey   **Hesperia High School, Hesperia**

OLD FASHIONED PRALINE PECAN ROLLS

Makes 12 rolls

1 loaf (1 lb.) Bridgford Frozen Bread Ready-Dough
½ cup butter or margarine, melted
¼ cup brown sugar

½ cup pecan halves
Filling:
⅔ cup pecans, chopped
½ cup brown sugar
2 tablespoons flour

Let Bridgford Frozen Bread Ready-Dough thaw until pliable. (Dough may be thawed overnight in the refrigerator or in the microwave oven for 6 minutes on low power). Place 4 tablespoons melted butter in bottom of a well greased 13 x 9" pan. Sprinkle ¼ cup brown sugar and ½ cup pecan halves over butter. On a lightly floured board, roll dough out to a 10 x 14" rectangle. Brush with 2 tablespoons melted butter. Combine filling ingredients and sprinkle evenly over dough. Beginning with 10" side, roll dough up tightly in jelly roll fashion. Pinch dough along edge to seal. Slice rolled dough into 12 pieces. Place slices, cut side down, in prepared pan. Brush dough with remaining butter. Let rise until rolls have doubled in size (2 to 3 hours). Bake at 350 degrees for 25 minutes or until golden brown. Carefully invert rolls onto serving platter at once (syrup is very hot!).

Bridgford Foods　　　　　　　　　　　　　　　**Anaheim, California**

Lighter Desserts

SUNBURST CHOCOLATE CAKE

Serves 12

3 eggs
¾ cup sugar
½ cup all purpose flour
⅓ cup unsweetened cocoa
½ teaspoon baking soda

¼ teaspoon salt
⅓ cup water
1 teaspoon vanilla
Citrus Filling (recipe follows)

Heat oven to 375 degrees. Grease sides and bottom of two 8" round pans; line bottoms with wax paper. In small mixer bowl, beat eggs for 3 minutes at high speed. Gradually add sugar; continue beating 2 minutes. Combine flour, cocoa, baking soda, and salt; add alternately with water and vanilla to egg mixture, folding gently until mixture is combined. Spread evenly in prepared pans. Bake 15 to 17 minutes or until top springs back when lightly touched in center. Cool 5 minutes; remove from pans and peel off paper. Cool completely. Prepare Citrus Filling. To assemble, place one cake layer on serving plate; spoon half citrus filling onto layer. Top with remaining layer and citrus filling. Garnish with reserved mandarin oranges. Chill several hours or overnight.

"120 calories per serving."

Citrus Filling:

1 envelope (1.3 oz.) whipped
   topping mix
½ cup cold 2% milk

1 can (11 oz.) mandarin orange
   segments, drained
¾ teaspoon orange peel, grated

In small mixer bowl, beat topping mix with milk until stiff peaks form, about 4 minutes. Reserve ½ cup orange segments for garnish; set aside. Cut remaining segments into thirds; gently fold orange peel and cut orange segments into topping.

Hershey Foods Corporation   **Hershey, Pennsylvania**

NO CHOLESTEROL CHOCOLATE CAKE

Makes one cake

2 cups flour
½ teaspoon salt
1 teaspoon baking powder
1 teaspoon baking soda
8 tablespoons cocoa

1 cup sugar
¾ cup lite or cholesterol-free
   mayonnaise
1 cup water
1 teaspoon vanilla

Mix together dry ingredients in a bowl. Add remaining ingredients and mix on high speed with electric mixer for 3 minutes. Pour into pan (one 9 x 13" or two 8" layers) sprayed with nonstick coating and bake at 350 degrees for 30 minutes.

"This is great when halved to bake in an 8" square pan for a small group. We also bake it in ice cream cones, 30 seconds each in the microwave; top with ice cream."

Linda Hubbs   **Lone Pine High School, Lone Pine**

EGGLESS, MILKLESS, BUTTERLESS CAKE

Serves 12

1¼ cups raisins or diced prunes
1¼ cups sugar
2 rounded tablespoons
  shortening
½ teaspoon salt
1¼ cups water

2 tablespoons cocoa
2 tablespoons cinnamon
2 cups flour
1 teaspoon soda
1 teaspoon vanilla
2 cups walnuts, chopped

Preheat oven to 325 degrees. In a large saucepan, bring these ingredients to a boil: raisins, sugar, shortening, salt, water, cocoa, and cinnamon. Allow to cool for 10 minutes. Stir in flour, soda, vanilla, and walnuts. Spread into a 9 x 13" cake pan. Bake for 20 minutes or until set.

"This is a recipe my husband's grandmother always makes. When I married him, he couldn't believe I didn't know how to make an "eggless, milkless, butterless" cake. Doesn't everyone!?"

DeLisa Davis   **Sutter High School, Sutter**

FRUITY PIZZA

Serves 12

1 pkg. (1 lb. 2 oz.) refrig. sugar
  cookie dough
⅓ cup sugar
1 pkg. (8 oz.) cream cheese
1 cup sour cream

½ teaspoon vanilla
any combination of fresh fruit
bananas, strawberries, grapes,
kiwi, peaches, berries, etc.

Cut dough into ⅛" slices. Line a 14" pizza pan with slices, overlapping slightly. Bake at 375 degrees, 12 minutes. Cool. Blend softened cream cheese, sour cream, sugar, and vanilla. Spread over cooled cookie crust. Arrange fruit slices over top. Chill at least 1 hour, serve.

"This recipe was shared by one of my dear students. It was a hit with everyone. It's a great summertime treat."

Laurie Larson   **Arcadia High School, Arcadia**

APPLE PIZZA

Serves 8

pie crust (prepared)
5 large apples
½ cup mozzarella or swiss cheese
½ cup walnuts
½ cup dark brown sugar

½ teaspoon cinnamon
½ teaspoon nutmeg
2 tablespoons butter or
   margarine

Preheat oven to 400 degrees. Grease a 12" pizza pan. Roll the pie crust into a 13" circle, place on greased pizza pan. Bake for 10 minutes. Peel, core and slice the apples into ¼-inch pieces, mix with sugar, cinnamon and nutmeg mixture. Spread cheese on crust then spread apples. Cut butter into small pieces and dot over the top. Bake 20 minutes. Cool and serve.

"11 grams of fat per slice."

Cindy Haulenbeck   **Letha Raney Int. School, Corona**

CARAMEL POPCORN

2 cups margarine
2 cups brown sugar
½ cup white corn syrup
½ teaspoon salt

½ teaspoon baking soda
8 quarts popped popcorn or
   1 cup unpopped popcorn

Mix the first four ingredients in a sauce pan and cook over medium heat for five minutes only. Add baking soda and stir well. Quickly, pour over popped popcorn. Use a large enough roasting pan to hold popcorn or a 9 x 13" pan using foil to build up the sides. (I have used many small pans.) It is not worth cutting this recipe in half, you're always wanting more! Bake at 250 degrees for one hour, stirring every 15 minutes.

Lynda Rasmussen   **Hughes Middle School, Long Beach**

BAKED APPLES

Serves 4

4 small baking apples
¼ cup unsweetened apple juice
1 cup water

1 teaspoon cinnamon
1 small orange, sliced
2 packets Equal sweetener

Preheat oven to 350 degrees. Core the apples and remove ¼ the top peel. Place apples in a shallow baking pan. Combine the water, juice, and cinnamon. Pour over the apples. Arrange the orange slices around the apples to help flavor the liquid. Cover the pan with aluminum foil and bake about 20 to 30 minutes or until fork tender. Remove from oven and sprinkle with Equal.

"Quick and easy. Your family and friends will like them. Only 83 calories per serving."

Tess Osborne   **Columbus Tustin Middle School, Tustin**

PINEAPPLE DESSERT

Serves 8

¼ cup butter
1½ cups powdered sugar
2 eggs, beaten
½ pound vanilla wafers

1 cup pineapple, crushed and
  drained
1 cup whipping cream, whipped,
  or 8 oz. Cool Whip

Cream butter and sugar till fluffy. Add egg and beat. Crush vanilla wafers and spread half on the bottom of a buttered 8" square glass dish. Then mix creamed mixture, pineapple, and whipped cream. Top with remaining crumbs. Chill overnight.

"Only 200 calories per serving."

Jill Burnham   **Bloomington High School, Bloomington**

LO-CAL LEMON CHEESECAKE

Serves 12

2 envelopes unflavored gelatin
¾ cup sugar
2 eggs, separated
1½ cups skim milk
1½ tablespoons lemon juice
1½ teaspoons lemon peel, grated

3 cups lowfat creamed cottage
  cheese
⅓ cup graham cracker crumbs
¼ teaspoon ground cinnamon
⅛ teaspoon ground nutmeg

In a medium saucepan, combine the unflavored gelatin and ½ cup sugar. Beat egg yolks with 1 cup milk. Add to gelatin. Stir over low heat until gelatin dissolves, about 5 minutes; add remaining ½ cup milk, lemon juice, and peel. In a large bowl, beat cottage cheese until smooth. Gradually add gelatin mixture to cottage cheese; mix well. Chill, stirring occasionally, until mixture mounds slightly when dropped from spoon. In a large bowl, beat egg whites until soft peaks form. Gradually add remaining ¼ cup sugar and beat until stiff. Fold in cheese mixture. Turn into 8 or 9" springform. Mix graham cracker crumbs, cinnamon, and nutmeg. Sprinkle on top of cheesecake. Chill until firm, at least 3 hours.

"A little more work than regular cheesecake recipes, but results are worth it. Approximately 150 calories per serving."

Sydney Fox   **Orange Glen High School, Escondido**

LITE STRAWBERRY CHOCOLATE PIE

Serves 6 to 8

6 oz. semisweet chocolate
2 tablespoons unsalted
 margarine
2 tablespoon cherry brandy

1½ pints strawberries
9" prepared pie shell
 (Mrs. Smith's, no sugar)

Melt chocolate pieces for 2 minutes in microwave. Add margarine and brandy; whisk until smooth. Pour into prebaked pie shell. Arrange strawberries on top, tips up. Refrigerate for 2 hours.

"May use regular margarine or regular pie shell. Calories will be the only difference. Using ingredients above, each slice has 190 calories."

Barbara Bressler   **Buena Park High School, Buena Park**

HIGH-LOW PINEAPPLE COTTAGE CHEESE DESSERT

Makes 12 servings

2 envelopes Knox gelatin
1 cup cold water
1 medium can crushed pineapple
1½ cups sugar

juice of 1 lemon
1 cup whipping cream *
1 cup cottage cheese

Soak gelatin in cold water; set aside. Cook pineapple, sugar, and lemon juice. Let boil about 10 minutes. Stir often. Pour pineapple mixture over dissolved gelatin and let cool. Whip cream (or egg white meringue mixture) and add to mixture. When this starts to thicken, add cottage cheese. Pour into a 9 x 13" pan. Chill until firm. Cut into squares and serve.
* Lower calorie substitute: 2 beaten egg whites plus 3 tablespoons sugar, beaten into a meringue

"This is called 'high-low' because it can be very rich or low calories. The low calorie version disappears just as fast."

Janet Griffith   **Norco High School, Norco**

CHOCOLATE-BANANA SHERBET

Makes 8 one-half cup servings

2 medium size ripe bananas
 (about 1 cup mashed)
1 cup apricot nectar, peach or
 pineapple juice, divided

½ cup semisweet chocolate chips
2 tablespoons sugar
1 cup milk

Slice bananas into blender container or food processor. Add ¾ cup fruit juice; blend until smooth. In small microwave-save bowl, combine chocolate chips, remaining fruit juice and sugar. Microwave at 100% high for 45 seconds. Whisk until chips are melted and mixture is smooth; add to mixture in blender. Blend until thoroughly combined. Add milk; blend until smooth. Pour into 9" square pan or two ice cube trays; freeze until hard around edges. Spoon mixture into large mixer bowl or food processor; process until smooth. Return to freezer; freeze about 2 hours; stir to break up ice crystals. Cover; freeze until firm. To serve, scoop into dessert dishes.

"130 calories per serving."

Hershey Foods Corporation   **Hershey, Pennsylvania**

CHOCOLATE DESSERT TIMBALES

Serves 6

1 envelope unflavored gelatin
½ cup cold water
6 tablespoons sugar
3 tablespoons unsweetened
   cocoa
1½ cups 2% milk

2 egg yolks
2 teaspoons vanilla extract
1 cup prepared whipped topping
   (8 calories per tablespoon)
fresh or canned fruit slices
   (low calorie)

In small bowl, sprinkle gelatin over cold water; set aside. In medium saucepan, combine sugar and cocoa; gradually stir in milk. Beat egg yolks slightly; add to saucepan. Cook over medium heat, stirring constantly, until mixture just begins to boil; remove from heat. Stir in gelatin and vanilla. Transfer to a bowl; chill, stirring occasionally, until mixture begins to set. Carefully fold whipped topping into chocolate mixture blending until smooth. Pour into 6 small custard cups; chill 1 to 2 hours or until set. Unmold and garnish as desired.

"133 calories per serving without garnish."

Hershey Foods Corporation   **Hershey, Pennsylvania**

WHIPPED BANANA PUDDING

Serves 8

½ teaspoon unflavored gelatin,
   softened in water
1 large banana, ripened
1 packet Equal

½ teaspoon lemon rind, grated
   (optional)
8 drops yellow food coloring
2 cups plain low fat yogurt

Blend all ingredients except yogurt into a blender until smooth. Fold in the yogurt. Pour into individual sherbet glasses. Chill well.

"I recently became a diabetic and am discovering some delicious sugar-free recipes. Only 52 calories per serving."

Tess Osborne   **Columbus Tustin Middle School, Tustin**

KAREN'S STRAWBERRIES JULIET

Serves 4

2½ cups fresh strawberries
⅓ cup frozen whipped topping,
thawed

⅓ cup plain yogurt
1 tablespoon sugar

Using fresh chilled strawberries, crush ¼ cup and halve the remaining ones; set aside. Combine crushed strawberries and remaining ingredients. Spoon halved strawberries into 4 sherbet glasses; top with strawberry yogurt mixture and serve immediately, or refrigerate.

"Only 78 calories per serving."

Angela Croce   **Mira Mesa High School, San Diego**

FROZEN YOGURT

1 package (16 oz.) strawberries,
frozen (no sugar added)
1 tablespoon lemon juice

1 cup plain yogurt
¼ cup powdered sugar
(optional)

Place all ingredients into food processor bowl and, using the metal blade, process until all fruit is processed and other ingredients are well blended. It is ready to serve immediately. Freeze any leftovers until later.

"Low in calories and yummy! Be creative and mix fruits together."

Marcia Nye   **Wilson High School, Long Beach**

APPLE CRISP

Serves 8 to 9

6 to 8 medium cooking apples
(peeled, cored, and quartered)
2 tablespoons lemon juice
1 cup quick oats, uncooked
¾ cup brown sugar, packed

½ cup flour
½ cup margarine, chilled and cut
into 6 pieces
1 teaspoon cinnamon

Preheat oven to 375 degrees. Slice apples in food processor; put into an ungreased 9" square baking pan. Sprinkle lemon juice over apples. Use food processor blade and process remaining ingredients until crumbly, about 10 seconds. Spread crumb mixture evenly over apples. Bake until apples are tender, about 40 to 45 minutes. Serve warm or cold, with or without ice cream or whipped cream.

"Quick, low calorie dessert that everyone likes."

Patty Dyle   **J.F. Kennedy High School, La Palma**

INDEX OF RECIPES

COOKIES

FRUITS AND GELATINS

ALPHABETIZED CONTRIBUTORS' LIST

AAA

Adams, Barbara, 51, 68
Merced HS-North Campus, Merced

Aiello, Joy, 50
Liberty HS, Brentwood

Alexis, Hazel G., 14
Thompson JHS, Bakersfield

Ali-Christie, Robin, 74
Nevada Union HS, Grass Valley

Amelotte, Pam, 10, 48
Ocean View HS, Huntington Beach

Anagnos, Maridel, 29, 101
Tokay HS, Lodi

Anderson, Jill Sweet, 55
Santa Paula Union HS, Santa Paula

Apple, Cheryle, 78
Rio Vista HS, Rio Vista

Armstead, Claudia, 57
Jefferson MS, Long Beach

BBB

Baczynski, Kathie, 37, 38
Mt. Carmel HS, San Diego

Banks, Judy, 28, 146
Temecula Valley HS, Temecula

Barnett, Linda, 19, 51
Matilija JHS, Ojai

Bass, Alcyone, 110
Lakewood HS, Lakewood

Bell, Lucille, 66, 94
Palmdale HS, Palmdale

Bennett, Karen, 86, 115
Norco HS, Norco

Black-Eacker, Ellen, 47
Nogales HS, La Puente

Blough, Shirley, 34, 42
Hillside JHS, Simi Valley

Bohte, Nancy, 28
So. Pasadena HS, So. Pasadena

Bradley, Amber, 56
El Capitan HS, Lakeside

Brayton, Linda, 98
Grace Davis HS, Modesto

Bressler, Barbara, 33, 156
Buena Park HS, Buena Park

Brown, Marjorie, 134, 137
Cabrillo HS, Lompoc

Brown, Susan, 52
Sowers MS, Huntington Beach

Bruce, Libby, 82
Troy HS, Fullerton

Bruce, Nancy, 31
San Juan HS, Citrus Heights

Brunell, Gail, 34
Leuzinger HS, Lawndale

Brunson, Nancy, 127
Arcata and McKinleyville HS,
McKinleyville

Burke, Brenda, 9, 132
Mt. Whitney HS, Visalia

Burkhart, Nancy, 149
Hueneme HS, Oxnard

Burnham, Jill, 155
Bloomington HS, Bloomington

Byrne, Betty, 130
Arroyo Grande HS, Arroyo Grande

CCC

Campbell, Theresa M., 113
J. F. Kennedy HS, La Palma

Carlson, Monica, 18, 37
La Contenta JHS, Yucca Valley

Castro, Diane, 77
Quartz Hill HS, Lancaster

Christopher, Janis, 132
Mt. Whitney HS, Visalia

Christy, Mary Ann, 39
Apple Valley HS, Apple Valley

Clark, Ginny, 26
Sonora HS, La Habra

Clements, Simone, 9, 144
Bret Harte HS, Altaville

Obermeyer, Lou, 127, 140
La Sierra HS, Riverside

OKeeffe, Alice, 133
Walnut HS, Walnut

Oliver, Jan, 123, 138
Irvine HS, Irvine

Osborne, Tess, 154, 157
Columbus Tustin MS, Tustin

Owen, Laurie, 81, 148
Hoover HS, San Diego

Oxford, Sally, 70, 79
Monache HS, Porterville

PPP

Panttaja, Virginia, 125
Sanger HS, Sanger

Paskins, Linda, 6, 95
Cordova Sr. HS, Rancho Cordova

Paul, Nan, 65
Grant MS, Escondido

Paulsin, Renee, 116
Hemet HS, Hemet

Pearl, Vicki A., 61
Giano JHS, La Puente

Pereira, Marilyn, 67
Hanford HS, Hanford

Phillips, Merlina, 137
McCloud HS, McCloud

Placido, Katie, 21, 129
Warren HS, Downey

Policy, Janet, 111
Ramona HS, Riverside

Priestley, Roberta, 129, 130
Alhambra HS, Alhambra

Pullan, Cheryl, 39, 55
Terrace Hills JHS, Grand Terrace

Putnam, Penny, 54
Divisadero MS, Visalia

RRR

Raglin, Tena, 56
Dos Palos HS, Dos Palos

Rasmussen, Lynda, 154
Hughes MS, Long Beach

Reece, Gloria, 41
Porterville HS, Porterville

Richmond, Mary E., 53
San Luis Obispo HS, San Luis Obispo

Roberson, Inez, 15
Correia JHS, San Diego

Robertson, Lynn, 131
Durham HS, Durham

Robertson, Sandy, 106
Whittier HS, Whittier

Robinson, Linda, 11, 63
Sinaloa JHS, Simi Valley

Rocheleau, Ginny, 93
Muirlands JHS, La Jolla

Rona, Nadean, 64
Columbus HS, Downey

Ross, Karen, 64
Demille MS, Long Beach

Rupp, Jackie, 73
Home Street MS, Bishop

Rupp, Janet, 94
El Rancho MS, Anaheim

SSS

Salau, Loretta, 133
Foothill HS, Bakersfield

Sarouhan, Olga, 29
Edison HS, Huntington Beach

Schletewitz, Ruth, 72
Roosevelt JHS, Kingsburg

Schneider, Laurine, 25
Downey HS, Downey

Sheats, Dianne, 54
Gridley HS, Gridley

Shelburne, Julie, 23, 70
Tulare Union HS, Tulare

Sheridan, Cari, 75
Grace Yokley JHS, Ontario

Silveira, Anne, 139
Central Valley HS, Central Valley

Simon, Diedre, 80
Norwalk HS, Norwalk

Skee, Charlotte, 125
San Clemente HS, San Clemente

Skidmore, Myra, 67
Downey HS, Downey

Slaughter, Sally, 147
Tehachapi HS, Tehachapi

Small, Donna A., 82
Santana HS, Santee

Smith, Bobbette, 16
Tokay HS, Lodi

Smith, Michelle, 28
Kraemer JHS, Placentia

Smith, Pat, 85, 109
Kern Valley HS, Lake Isabella

Sowell, Stacy, 25
Juniper Int. School, Palmdale

Springhorn, Mary, 12
Anderson Union HS, Anderson

Staffanson, Lura, 7, 36
Perris HS, Perris

Steele, Adrienne, 81, 143
Lee JHS, Woodland

Stinton, Judy, 100
Mt. Miguel HS, Spring Valley

Stubblefield, Jeri Lynn, 15
Lemoore HS, Lemoore

Sullivan, Susan, 146
Caruthers HS, Caruthers

Swearingen, Myrna, 49, 71
Corona HS, Corona

Swennes, Donna, 97
El Capitan HS, Lakeside

TTT

Tam, Marilyn, 121, 125
Orange Glen HS, Escondido

Tice, Becky, 67
Dana Hills HS, Dana Point

Tilson, Karen, 110, 128
Poly HS, Riverside

Topham, Carleen, 4
Dexter JHS, Whittier

Topp, Judi, 38
Alder JHS, Fontana

Traw, Marianne, 91, 124
Ball JHS, Anaheim

Turner, Sharon, 120
El Dorado HS, Placentia

Tyree, Sonja, 77
Ruben Ayala HS, Chino

UUU

Umbro, Brenda, 74
San Pasqual HS, Escondido

WWW

Walker, Gloria, 27, 128
Casa Roble Fundamental HS, Orangevale

Walters, Sue, 92
Morse HS, San Diego

Warren, Barbara, 143
Colton HS, Colton

Waterbury, Sue, 16
San Luis Obispo HS, San Luis Obispo

Wells, Betty, 88
Oroville HS, Oroville

West, Olga Erickson, 105
Santana and West Hills HS, Santee

Wetzel, Naomi, 19
Delta HS, Clarksburg

Willis, Marty, 135, 139
Poway HS, Poway

Wilson, Dorothy, 13, 26
Dale JHS, Anaheim

Winzenread, Linda, 7, 99
Whittier HS, Whittier

Wong, Pat, 30
Taft HS, Taft

Woolley, Linda, 9
La Sierra HS, Riverside

Worland, Janet, 101
Silver Valley HS, Yermo

ZZZ

Desserts For The Nineties
California Cookbook Company
1115 Sheppard Drive
Fullerton, CA 92631

Please send_____ copy(ies) of your cookbook at $8.95 each (includes tax and postage). Make checks payable to: *California Cookbook Company.*

Enclosed is my check for $_____.

Name_____

Street_____

City_____ State_____ Zip_____

Desserts For The Nineties
California Cookbook Company
1115 Sheppard Drive
Fullerton, CA 92631

Please send_____ copy(ies) of your cookbook at $8.95 each (includes tax and postage). Make checks payable to: *California Cookbook Company.*

Enclosed is my check for $_____.

Name_____

Street_____

City_____ State_____ Zip_____

Desserts For The Nineties
California Cookbook Company
1115 Sheppard Drive
Fullerton, CA 92631

Please send_____ copy(ies) of your cookbook at $8.95 each (includes tax and postage). Make checks payable to: *California Cookbook Company.*

Enclosed is my check for $_____.

Name_____

Street_____

City_____ State_____ Zip_____